"In the field of interpretation ⟨...⟩ simply no one as expert as ⟨...⟩, Body Language, confirms he ⟨...⟩ subject. This book is a must for everybody!"

Libby Appel, Artistic Director Emerita at Oregon Shakespeare Festival

"Whether you are a manager, a recruiter, a sales person, a candidate or a client, Kuhnke's book is essential reading. It takes a complex subject and renders it accessible to all."

John Lucy, HR Director at Berwin Leighton Paisner LLP

"Body Language is essential reading for anyone who wants to really understand people beyond words. Whether you're trying to decode corporate politics, or get on with the in-laws – I would highly recommend this book."

John Kelly, Off Trade Director at Heineken Ireland

"To rely on words alone is like viewing the world through the wrong end of a telescope. Expand your appreciation of all language a person brings to a conversation. This book will help you decode the non-verbal signals that posture and expression bring to the dialogue."

Russell Hampshire FCA

"A real hands-on guide that helped me to understand the messages my body sends and then taught me how to align them with my verbal communication. It also serves very well to interpret other people's emotions. If you care about relationships reading this book is a must."

Günter Schäuble, Head of Corporate Finance & Tax at Schindler Group, Switzerland

"If you are looking for a book that combines the theory of body language with insightful exercises and techniques that you can practice yourself, then this is the book for you. *Body Language* comprehensively reveals the most important information on nonverbal communication that everybody should learn."

Kasia Wezowski, co-founder of The Centre for Body Language

"Straightforward, accessible, and filled with useful tips and exercises, this book is a 'must have' for HR professionals and business leaders."

Emma Lyon, Fellow CIPD and International HR Director

"Clear, congruent communication – in which your body language matches your spoken words – is vital if you want people to understand your message. Elizabeth's tips and exercises are simple, practical and easy to implement. I highly recommend this book."

Beverley Sorsby, Head of Human Resources, Professional Services

BODY
LANGUAGE

Learn how to read others
and communicate with
confidence

Elizabeth Kuhnke

Illustrations by Curtis Allen

CAPSTONE
A Wiley Brand

This edition first published 2016
© 2016 Elizabeth Kuhnke

Registered office
John Wiley and Sons Ltd, The Atrium, Southern Gate, Chichester, West Sussex, PO19 8SQ, United Kingdom

For details of our global editorial offices, for customer services and for information about how to apply for permission to reuse the copyright material in this book please see our website at www.wiley.com.

The right of the author to be identified as the author of this work has been asserted in accordance with the Copyright, Designs and Patents Act 1988.

Wiley publishes in a variety of print and electronic formats and by print-on-demand. Some material included with standard print versions of this book may not be included in e-books or in print-on-demand. If this book refers to media such as a CD or DVD that is not included in the version you purchased, you may download this material at http://booksupport.wiley.com. For more information about Wiley products, visit www.wiley.com.

Designations used by companies to distinguish their products are often claimed as trademarks. All brand names and product names used in this book and on its cover are trade names, service marks, trademark or registered trademarks of their respective owners. The publisher and the book are not associated with any product or vendor mentioned in this book. None of the companies referenced within the book have endorsed the book.

Limit of Liability/Disclaimer of Warranty: While the publisher and author have used their best efforts in preparing this book, they make no representations or warranties with the respect to the accuracy or completeness of the contents of this book and specifically disclaim any implied warranties of merchantability or fitness for a particular purpose. It is sold on the understanding that the publisher is not engaged in rendering professional services and neither the publisher nor the author shall be liable for damages arising herefrom. If professional advice or other expert assistance is required, the services of a competent professional should be sought.

Library of Congress Cataloging-in-Publication Data
Names: Kuhnke, Elizabeth, author.
Title: Body language : learn how to read others and communicate with
    confidence / Elizabeth Kuhnke.
Description: Hoboken : Capstone, 2016.
Identifiers: LCCN 2016012012 (print) | LCCN 2016016289 (ebook) |
    ISBN 9780857087041 (paperback) | ISBN 9780857087072 (ebk) |
    ISBN 9780857087034 (ebk) | ISBN 9780857087072 (pdf) | ISBN 9780857087034 (epub)
Subjects: LCSH: Body language.
Classification: LCC BF637.N66 K8397 2016 (print) | LCC BF637.N66 (ebook) |
    DDC 153.6/9–dc23
LC record available at https://lccn.loc.gov/2016012012

A catalogue record for this book is available from the British Library.

ISBN 978-0-857-08704-1 (paperback)
ISBN 978-0-857-08707-2 (ebk)   ISBN 978-0-857-08703-4 (ebk)

Cover design: Wiley   Cover image: © Toby Bridson/iStockphoto
Illustrations by Curtis Allen

Set in 9.5/13pt ITC Franklin Gothic Std by Aptara, New Delhi, India
Printed in Great Britain by TJ International Ltd, Padstow, Cornwall, UK

CONTENTS

INTRODUCTION

"When the eyes say one thing, and the tongue another,
a practiced man relies on the language of the first."

Ralph Waldo Emerson

You're probably familiar with this scenario: someone is saying one thing to you, while their body seems to be saying something else – and you're left feeling confused. Do you believe the spoken words you're hearing or the body language that you're seeing? Global research and anecdotal evidence consistently show that the truth lies in the manner of delivery.

Not that words don't matter. They do. But if the words and the delivery don't match, your listeners are going to believe what they observe rather than what you're saying.

"Without uttering a syllable, you can convey your thoughts, feelings, and intentions through your body language."

While your spoken words convey information like facts and data, your body reveals other information like your attitude, intentions, and general state of being. And, while you may tell a white lie or two to save someone's feelings, or may create total fabrications to protect your interests, don't be surprised if your body gives the game away. For example, let's say that a colleague is given the job that you wanted and you say "I'm happy for you". The only problem is: your eyes are squinted, your brow is furrowed, and your fists are clenched. Your words are saying one thing while your body is saying something else. No wonder your co-worker turns away in disappointment or even worse, disgust.

However, all is not lost. By being aware of the messages your body sends out, and by practising specific gestures, postures, and expressions, you can create the impressions and convey the messages that you want to communicate. In addition, by observing and interpreting other people's actions, you have the upper hand when it comes to understanding their mindset and responding to their behaviour.

> "I pretended to be somebody I wanted to be until I finally became that person."
>
> *–Cary Grant*

So, if you want to enhance your interpersonal communication, learning how to read other people's body language and being able to control the signs and signals that your gestures, posture, and facial expressions transmit is vital. Restated: *If relationships matter to you, if you want to know what people are thinking, and if you want to determine how people perceive you, learn about body language*. The more conscious you are of unspoken messages, the better equipped you will be to build relationships, anticipate reactions, and adapt your behaviour according to the environment.

Learning how body language works and how you can perfect yours takes commitment. To test your level of interest, start by asking yourself the following questions:

- Am I willing to accept that my posture, movements, and facial expressions have an effect on others?
- Am I willing to understand that my mood affects my behaviour and other people's reactions to me?
- Do I want to communicate with authenticity, clarity, and confidence?
- Am I willing to practise?

If you answered "Yes" to any or all of these questions, read on. Even if you responded "No", the fact that you've gotten this far indicates that you're interested enough in non-verbal behaviour to persevere. Who knows? By practising the suggestions I share with you, you could become an expert at conveying and interpreting the unspoken messages behind the spoken word.

RECOGNIZING AND INTERPRETING PHYSICAL SIGNS AND SIGNALS TAKES PRACTICE

Throughout this book you will discover the meanings behind postures, movements, gestures, and facial expressions. You will learn how to decipher lies and demonstrate courting behaviour. You will learn both how to clarify your messages as well as camouflage what you'd rather not reveal. Before going any further, remember to *approach the study of body language with respect and responsibility*.

- **Consider the context.** Counting on one gesture to convey an entire meaning is about as sensible as counting on one word to tell an entire story.
- **Avoid commenting on what you observe.** Unless someone asks for feedback on his/her behaviour, keep your observations to yourself. Making negative comments about what you notice could lead to unfortunate consequences.

66 Read the signs. Reflect on what they mean. React appropriately. 99

LOOK FOR CLUSTERS OF GESTURES BEFORE MAKING A DECLARATION OF MEANING OR INTENT

If someone says "I love you" with a cleaver-like frown line between the eyes, clenched fists, a curled lip, and flared nostrils, you might want to run away as fast as possible. If, however, the nostrils are flared while the mouth is partially open with a smile playing at the lips, the hands are open with the palms facing you, and the eyes are moist, you'd be right in recognizing the signs of sexual interest.

When you say "I've never been happier" with dull eyes and slumped shoulders, don't be surprised if your listener asks you, "What's wrong?" There's no point in getting angry or denying that your words are saying one thing while your non-verbal behaviours are communicating something else.

"I've never been happier" – who do you believe?

WHAT'S IN IT FOR ME?

At this point, you might still be wondering why you should concern yourself with learning how to read other people's body language. You might be deliberating the importance of identifying different types of gestures, postures, and expressions. You might even be questioning the benefit of adapting your behaviour to suit the moment. If that's the case, consider the following scenarios.

Perhaps you want to know how your boss feels about your current performance, or are curious about what your partner is thinking. Perhaps you want to impress a potential employer or reject a possible suitor. *When you observe and interpret other people's body language, you gain access to their state of mind.* The more you know what others are thinking and how they're feeling, the more you will be able to choose how to react towards them.

❝ If you want to create positive and productive relationships, being adept at reading the signs and adapting your behaviour is your gateway to success. ❞

In addition, if you want to communicate your feelings without speaking, letting your body do the talking is the way to go. For example, you and your colleague can agree that when either of you puts an index finger by the side of their nose that means "stop talking". You can set up a series of signals that indicate the time has come to leave the room. You can suggest your interest in someone through the way you look at them, without committing yourself verbally in case the interest isn't reciprocated. Your body language can speak for you.

THE YODA SYSTEM

Years ago, one of my teachers suggested the following system for transmitting, reading, and responding to non-verbal communication. She named it YODA, as in the Jedi Master. If you're serious about learning how to read and respond to others' body language, and if you want to enhance your ability to communicate effectively through your movements and facial expressions, this method is a good one to follow.

You

- Accept responsibility for the impact of your non-verbal behaviours.
- Accept that your feelings, moods, and emotions impact on the signals you emit and those that you, in turn, receive.

Observe

- Practise conscious observation.
- Increase the amount of detail you observe.

Decode

- Identify other people's physical behaviours.
- Choose your best response.

Adapt

- Adapt your behaviours to convey your intended messages.
- Adapt your responses to other people's signals.

You can apply this system whenever you want to interpret and respond to others' non-verbal behaviours. In addition, the structure offers you the opportunity to identify your own behaviours and the impact they might have.

WHERE TO BEGIN?

In order to make this book relevant to your daily life, I have structured the content around specific scenarios. This way you can flip to the section that is relevant for you without having to search through material that may not be germane to your needs. Each section identifies detailed actions that you can expect to encounter and provides you with examples of effective behaviours you can adopt in response. In addition, at the end of each chapter you will find exercises designed to enhance your ability to communicate through the use of your gestures, movements, and facial expressions.

If you want to improve your ability to read other people's feelings and intentions, or develop your ability to reveal – or conceal – your own, you'll find the answers here. *In a nutshell, the purpose of this book is to help you recognize the power of body language and turn you into a top-notch communicator.*

Now, turn to a section that interests you and start reading.

1

WHAT YOUR BODY LANGUAGE SAYS ABOUT YOU

"There's language in her eye, her cheek, her lip,
Nay, her foot speaks; her wanton spirits look out
At every joint and motive of her body."

William Shakespeare

Feeling hot, engaged, and passionate? Feeling low, aloof, and cool? You don't need to answer that question. Your body says it all.

Standing proud and strutting your stuff indicates that you're ready and raring to go, while slumping your shoulders and shuffling your feet shows that you're carrying a heavy load. Hanging out on the sidelines with your arms crossed, a frown on your face, and your head burrowed into your chest suggests you're suspiciously watchful; meanwhile, engaging with a group of people, using open gestures and animated expressions, implies that you're prepared to party.

THE INNER AND OUTER CONNECTION

What you might find interesting about non-verbal behaviour – and body language in particular – is the relationship between **values, beliefs, attitudes** – and **gestures, facial expressions, posture.**

For example:

If *openness* is important to someone, you can expect to see that **value** reflected in free, approachable, and receptive movements and facial expressions. If they value *privacy*, their body language is more closed and contained.

If you hold the **belief** that you're unworthy, insignificant, and somehow "lacking", you might (1) overcompensate by being loud, brash, and seeking attention; or (2) withdraw, physically cave in on yourself, and avoid engaging with others. On the contrary, if you believe that you're an okay person, you will likely greet other people with warmth, curiosity, and generosity.

If your **attitude** is "I can't be bothered", your facial expressions are slack and your movements lack spontaneity. When you embrace a "Go, get 'em!" attitude, your body bursts with liveliness. Smiles surge across your face and you fist-pump the air as you jump for joy. Or a modified version of that.

In addition, consider the connection between **feelings and behaviour**. Whether you're conscious of them or not, your **emotions, moods** and **state of mind** play out in the way your body moves.

For instance, feeling **upbeat and wanting to spread the love**? Note your gestures and facial expressions: smiling, open, with a spring in your step and a sparkle in your eye. Feeling **downbeat and demoralized**? Look at yourself now: limp, bowed, with little sign of life.

> **"Even if you're trying to hide what you're experiencing, little leakages, "tells", and mini micro expressions give the game away every time."**

Little Things Mean A Lot

A client asked me to join her while she interviewed a potential member of her leadership team. Both when she asked the candidate about his contribution to the success of the previous team he led and what value he could bring to the organization, I observed micro expressions flash across his face and body movements that indicated a high level of defensiveness. These consisted of:

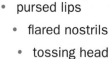

- pursed lips
- flared nostrils
- tossing head and casting sky shots
- forced laughter
- fake smile
- shifting in his seat
- jiggling feet
- pulling backwards into his seat while crossing his arms and legs and tilting his head sideways.

Although the facial expressions were fleeting, they were telling, as were his body movements and gestures. Together, they conveyed the message that he was feeling the pressure. And, no surprise... Turns out that the candidate wasn't all he claimed to be.

Had my client not trusted my observations, she could have made an expensive mistake. While he told a good tale – spinning and exaggerating here and there – his body's movements told a truer story.

Not even your **thoughts and intentions** are immune to reflecting themselves in your movements and facial expressions. For example, your boss says something that you **think** is the stupidest thing you've ever heard. Before you know it, your eyes are rolling around in your head, which is the rudest facial expression a person can display, next to gagging. At that point, you might consider looking for a new job, as you may have blotted your copy book by demonstrating your derision and disdain.

Another example. You see someone who catches your attention. And you catch theirs. Observe how your bodies speak. Your eyes connect and hold the gaze. Your lips slide into shy, sensuous, inviting smiles. Your chests and chins may lift as your bodies tilt forward, all of which indicate that your **intention** is to get to know one another.

"It's amazing how many things you can do when you're just pretending."

–Kim Gordon

Applying the "As If" Principle

Frequently, clients ask me to help them develop and project **confidence**. From the C-suite to the up and coming stars, confidence is the number one quality they all want to possess. No matter how successful they are at their day jobs, each one has a little voice inside their heads telling them that they're not very good at demonstrating, for instance:

- poise
- assertiveness
- self-assurance.

Frequently they ask me how they can convey:

- calmness in a crisis
- conviction
- courage.

I tell them, "Act as if."

According to the "as if" principle, you can create whatever state you desire by acting "as if" you already have what you would like to have. Like a child at play, you pretend to be who – or what – you want to be. And bingo! Before you know it, you've convinced yourself and others that you are, in this instance, **confident**.

66 When you act "as if" you create a new reality for yourself. 99

The irony is, you don't even have to experience the feelings that go with the mental state you want to project, which is good news if, for example, you're feeling doubtful and you want to convey certainty. As long as you act "as if", the rest takes care of itself.

Basic behaviours that demonstrate confidence include the following.

- **Posture.** Upright, chest expanded, head lifting upwards from the crown, chin held in a horizontal position, the sensation that the shoulder blades are meeting at the spinal cord and melting downward. Weight evenly distributed.

- **Eye contact.** When speaking, look at the other person 45–75% of the time. When listening, aim for 65–85%. Too much eye contact can make a person look defensive or threatening. Too little indicates signs of discomfort, including shame or shyness.

- **Facial expressions.** Think "Calm. Open. Positive." A warm smile welcomes others into your arena and makes you appear in control of your environment. Avoid big, toothy grins, as they can make you appear more comic-like than confident.

- **Gestures.** Contain your gestures. Be in command of your movements. Keep them simple and clear. Gesturing higher than the shoulders implies a lack of control, while gesturing below the waist indicates a lack of interest.

Once you take on the behaviours that demonstrate confidence, you'll be amazed what happens. The more you act "as if", the more others react to you as if that's who you really are. The more they react positively towards you, the more you feel comfortable with the behaviours.

As your feelings change, so does your thinking; and as your thinking changes, so do your behaviours. The cycle of thoughts, behaviours, and feelings comes full circle.

For an excellent, short YouTube video that demonstrates this principle, go to https://www.youtube.com/watch?v=Ngr2kG48Xvw

Be advised: while the behaviours listed above are acknowledged as being those that confident people demonstrate, we are all different and therefore may have variations on how we project confidence. Whichever behaviours you choose, make sure that they are true to who you are and what you stand for.

> **"When you act "as if", you take on the behaviours of the state you want to project in order to create your desired outcomes. "**

READING PEOPLE'S EMOTIONS

"In this respect, I suppose I'm the total opposite of Garry [Kasparov]. With his very emotive body language at the [chess] board he shows and displays all his emotions. I don't."

–*Vladimir Kramnik*

Some people wear their feelings on their sleeves and act out what they're experiencing at the time. Others choose to suppress their moods in an effort to conceal their feelings. When you're **deciphering other people's emotions**, remember the following:

- Look for clusters.
- Read body language in context.
- Some non-verbal behaviour is culture specific.
- Observe what's happening in the present.
- Don't judge what you notice based on past experience.
- Treat the other person with respect.

Many body-language signals can imply negative states, such as

- boredom
- disinterest
- anxiety
- uncertainty.

This can lead you to believe that the person is tired, fed up, or feeling out of their depth. And you're probably right. That being said, before making your final interpretation, ask yourself: "What is happening that is causing the negative feelings, resulting in the negative behaviour?"

For instance, it might be due to a disrespectful boss, work overload, fatigue, feeling excluded, hunger, illness, change, etc. While non-verbal behaviour is a sure indicator of a person's state of mind, circumstances play a part too. Whatever you do, don't jump to conclusions based on a single movement, gesture, or facial expression. Body language is best interpreted in clusters and in context.

Throughout this book, you can find specific **signs and signals to watch for**. I've included a few more below, which, when taken in context, are a reliable indicator of a person's mental state.

Signs of negative states

- Sweating.
- Flushed skin.
- Chewing on objects, including lips and fingers.
- Jiggling feet.
- Shallow breathing.
- Frowning.
- Tense lips.
- Short, quick breaths.
- Contracted pupils.

Signs of positive states

- Cool skin.
- Open gestures.
- Calm demeanour.
- Genuine smiles.
- Easy eye contact.
- Deep breathing.

Moods, attitudes, and emotions reveal themselves through your non-verbal behaviours. Even if you want to conceal your

feelings or intentions, a twitch of your cheek, the widening –
or narrowing – of your eyes, and the turn of your lips will
give your game away. If you want to project a specific state
of mind – let's say, feeling calm, confident, and in control –
take on the corresponding behaviours and pretend that you
are what you want to be. Before you know it, not only will
you have convinced others, you might even have convinced
yourself.

Recall a time when you felt confident. Imagine yourself in that state now, evoking every aspect you can remember. When practising this exercise, place yourself in the present, rather than the past, to make the state real in the here and now.

How are you demonstrating confidence in your behaviour?
- How are you holding your head?
- What is your posture like?
- What gestures and facial expressions are you using?

How are you feeling?
- What is your breathing rate?
- What is your body temperature?

What are you hearing?
- What does your voice sound like?
- What are others saying about you?

What are you seeing?
- Describe your skin tone and colour.
- What do you notice about your environment?

The more detail you can summon up, the more able you will be to recreate your desired state.

2

LISTENING

"Listening is a positive act: you have to put yourself out to do it."

David Hockney

I f you thought that listening was a passive act, you're mistaken. Listening requires energy, care, and attention. Listening is the greatest gift you can give to someone. When you listen to other people, you make them feel valued. You're showing that you are interested in what they have to say. And when people feel that you're interested in them and value them as individuals, they become your biggest supporters.

When I was a little girl, my mother told me that God gave me two eyes, two ears, and one mouth. By observing more and speaking less, I'd gain valuable information that would give me the edge over others.

> ❝ **People who speak more than they listen miss valuable information.** ❞

WHAT IS ACTIVE LISTENING?

Eyes

Ears

Undivided Attention

Heart

The Chinese Symbol for Active Listening includes symbols for Ears, Eyes, and Heart as well as for Undivided Attention.

When listening actively, you engage your eyes, ears, and heart. You focus on the other person, giving them your undivided attention. You listen to understand, and leave judgements outside the door.

Listening requires more than just hearing the words being spoken. When you're deeply engaged and really listening to someone you not only pay attention to the words themselves, but also observe the non-verbal behaviours as well. These include (but are not limited to) the following.

Facial Expressions

> "He had the look of one who had drunk the cup of life and found a dead beetle at the bottom."
>
> *–P.G. Wodehouse*

Look to a person's face if you want to know their mood, thoughts, and intentions.

Forehead

- Smooth indicates calmness.
- Wrinkled displays worry, concern, annoyance, or anger.

Eyes

- Comfortable, easy eye contact shows a relaxed attitude.
- Staring or avoiding eye contact suggests a negative state of mind.

Mouth

- Tightly drawn or pursed lips are a sign of a negative mindset.
- Chewing or sucking on lips implies unease or discomfort.
- Lips that are lifted in a smile indicate a positive outlook.

Skin colour and temperature

- Flushed and moist skin reveals stress and tension.
- Cool, dry skin indicates a relaxed state.

Having noted the behaviours, and determined their meaning, you're prepared to choose your response.

Gestures

> "The most important thing in communication is hearing what isn't being said. The art of reading between the lines is a life long quest of the wise."
> –Shannon L. Alder

Whether gestures are conscious or not, they reveal vital signs for understanding the speaker's attitude and intentions. For example:

- Short, sharp, jerky gestures imply tension and aggression.
- Fluid, open, slow gestures suggest receptiveness and affability.
- Fiddling fingers denote fretfulness.
- Fingers held in the steeple position at waist level in front of the body indicate power, influence, and authority.
- Clenched fists indicate anger or frustration.

- Crossed arms indicate detachment.
- Jiggling feet and tapping toes show impatience.
- A balanced body reflects a controlled mindset.
- Clenched fists, a laser stare, and tightly drawn lips in combination indicate a threatening attitude.
- A trembling lip, bowed head, and moist eyes are signs of sadness.
- Finger picking, lip chewing, and neck rubbing reveal discomfort.

Vocal Patterns

Placement, pace, and volume are vocal qualities that reveal a person's state of mind.

- A strangled sound, stuck in a person's throat, is a sign that the speaker is holding back, demonstrating lack of clarity, freedom, and commitment.
- High-pitched, tight voices come across as childlike, uncertain, and insecure.
- A voice that resonates from the chest implies authority.
- Voices that are flat, muffled, and lacking in resonance indicate that the speaker is avoiding engaging in open communication.
- Rushed sentences and garbled words indicate anxiety.
- A loud voice demonstrates dominance and control.
- A soft voice can indicate insecurity and a lack of engagement.

Breathing Patterns

Where you place your breathing impacts on how you communicate and are perceived.

- Quick, short, shallow breaths denote angst, anxiety, and anger. The sound produced is either fearful, weak, lacking in support when placed in the upper throat, or harsh, angry, and strangled when produced lower down the vocal channel.

- Breathing from the diaphragm produces a rich, round sound. Long, deep breaths that rise from the bowels of your belly are strong and solid. Your voice resonates, eliciting attention and respect.

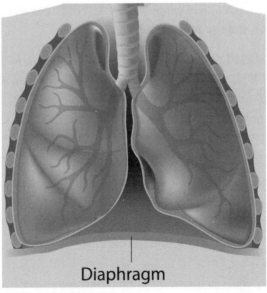

Diaphragm

Breathe from the diaphragm to produce a rich, round sound.

Sourced from Shutterstock (Wiley) 119606584 (Wiley Credit – Alila Medical Media/Shutterstock)

Word Choice

People perceive and respond to the world around them in different ways.

Some people are **visual**, peppering their communication with words and phrases, like: "See. Look. Point of view. The way I see this is... Can you see this from my perspective? I envision this project... I'm a big picture person. The outlook for next quarter is good."

Others experience the world through sound. People with a preference for the **auditory** use phrases such as: "How does that sound to you? That's music to my ears. I hear you. We're singing from the same song sheet. We're in tune with each other."

Those who are more attuned to touch are said to be **kinaesthetic**. They use language like: "How do you feel about that? Let's touch base. Let's strike a balance before this becomes even more uncomfortable. The thought turns my blood cold."

Speakers may use a combination of senses when speaking. Your job, as listener, is to pick up on the speaker's language and reflect it back in your response. Understanding the speaker's point of view enables you to respond to what you hear in a way the speaker can relate to. Even if your preferences are different, if you want to establish rapport and demonstrate good listening skills, adapt your language when necessary to match the other person's. (In Chapter 3, you will learn more about establishing rapport.)

Posture

When people aren't physically engaged there's little chance of listening taking place.

Standing, sitting, or lying down, how you position your body impacts on your readiness, ability, and willingness to listen.

- Slouched, slumped bodies indicate a lack of engagement and a lack of interest.
- Lifting your torso, allowing your head to sit upright on your neck while letting your shoulders lie back and down, and looking at the person speaking, with a calm expression on your face, sends out signs that you're interested and prepared to listen.

LISTEN FOR WHAT'S *NOT* BEING SAID

While you may find this suggestion counterintuitive, play with the idea: *Listen for what's not being said*. For example, someone tells you that their life is super fantastic. But something in their delivery tells a different story. Perhaps their eyes are dull or watery, maybe their lower lip is trembling. You might notice that their voice is flat and lifeless, or that their hands are hanging limp and their head is hanging down. Non-verbal signs reveal more about a person's internal state than the words they speak.

 F-I-N-E

John had had a tough day. He was struggling to meet a work deadline, he and his wife had had a row that morning, and he had received some harsh criticism from a colleague. On his way out of the office, he bumped into his boss, Maggie – a woman known for her perception, wit, and straight talk. Maggie noticed that John was looking stressed and asked him how he was feeling. Forcing a smile onto his face, John replied: "Oh, I'm fine, thanks." To which Maggie quietly responded, leaning towards him with a gentle smile on her face: "Fine? As in fed up, insecure, neurotic, and enraged?" Reading the negative tension in John's body – including tight lips, hunched shoulders, and a furrowed brow – gave Maggie an insight into John's true mental state, despite what he said. She, in turn, was able to adapt her behaviour to demonstrate her care and understanding.

66 **By paying attention to their choice of words and means of delivery, you can read the speaker's mood and adapt your behaviour accordingly.** 99

While taking in all of the above information may seem a daunting task, the more you practise, the more you will improve.

When you listen to someone, giving them your complete attention, you make them feel **valued** and that what they're saying is **important**. Even if you don't want to hear what they have to say, act as if you do. Instead of arguing and justifying – thus shutting down the listening process – breathe deeply, calm your face and body, look at the other person as they speak, and smile. When you adopt the attitude and behaviours of an interested listener, you will find that your engagement levels rise. (Turn back to Chapter 1 for more about acting "as if".)

> "When you really listen to another person from their point of view, and reflect back to them that understanding, it's like giving them emotional oxygen."
>
> *–Stephen Covey*

TIPS FOR HELPING YOU LISTEN

- Open your eyes and aim to look at the other person 65–85% of the time while they're speaking. Avoid staring, as doing so could make the other person feel uncomfortable.
- Lean in slightly towards the other person while they're speaking. Nod your head to let them know that you think what they're saying makes sense. By nodding you also encourage the other person to continue speaking.
- Smile to demonstrate that you value them. A simple lifting of the sides of your mouth, a full-blown grin – whichever is appropriate for the situation.

- If you want to make yourself appear concerned or compassionate, slightly tilt your head. Avoid frowning as that will make you look as though you disagree or are finding fault.

- If you want the speaker to carry on, open-handed gestures in combination with leaning in and nodding your head encourage the speaker to continue, enabling you to observe further.

- Use reassuring phrases like "Tell me more", "I see", "Then what happened?" to encourage the other person to keep speaking.

- If you have a tendency to interrupt when someone else is speaking, shut your mouth. Literally, shut your mouth. With your lips sealed, you can't interject. Be careful not to clench your teeth as that will cause tension in your jaw as well as in your mind. And if your mind is tense you'll find listening more challenging than if your brain is open to new information.

To become a good listener, make a conscious habit of noticing people's non-verbal behaviours and word choices. Rather than trying to take in everything at once, start slowly.

For example, one day you might choose to observe a person's facial expressions in combination with word choice and speed of delivery. The next day you might choose tone of voice, gestures, and posture. And so on. Because this exercise requires concentration when you begin, be careful to treat the people that you're observing in a respectful way. Let them know what you're doing and your reasons why (for example, because you want to improve your communication skills).

The more you practise, the more fluid your listening skills will become. Eventually, your intuition will take over and you'll be reading, reflecting, and responding to what you observe without consciously thinking about what you're doing.

3

BUILDING RAPPORT AND NETWORKING

"Many believe effective networking is done face-to-face, building a rapport with someone by looking at them in the eye, leading to a solid connection and foundational trust."

Raymond Arroyo

The people who achieve success in their careers, the people to whom others flock and want to emulate, the people who seek solid connections and build relationships based on trust… these are the people who use their rapport-building and networking skills to advance their agendas. No matter how bright, capable, and appropriate for the job you are, if you don't reveal those traits in your behaviour, no one's going to know or care about knowing you.

The best rapport builders and networkers are **curious**. They want to know about **you**. Listen to the kinds of questions they ask:

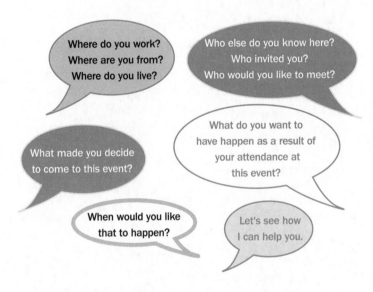

You may be thinking "Whoa. Those are pretty personal questions" and you'd be right. But, if you don't ask the questions, you don't get the answers. The more you know about someone, the better positioned you are to build rapport and network with them. By demonstrating interest and a desire to help others, you will become a five-star networker.

You can gain useful information by asking open questions – those that require more than a "yes" or "no" answer.

> "It's all about people. It's about networking and being nice to people and not burning any bridges. Your book is going to impress, but in the end it is people that are going to hire you."
>
> *–Mike Davidson*

Being nice to people and not burning any bridges. Sounds simple enough. So, how come some people find being nice so difficult? Why do others destroy relationships? Those are topics for another book. For now, observe how people who are *not being nice* behave. Their:

- eyes tend to squint
- mouths purse or pucker
- lips turn down
- chins thrust forward
- foreheads lower
- face frowns
- arms are crossed
- gestures are closed.

Adopt a couple of those positions for a few moments and see how you feel. Because the way you behave impacts on how you feel, the chances are you're feeling quite negative. And, because how you feel and behave influence other people's reactions to you, don't be surprised if you find yourself standing on your own. Negative attitudes and behaviours are guaranteed to push people away from you. Not good for rapport building and networking.

Part of the point of rapport building and networking is to put others at ease. Do that and you'll discover that when your name comes up in conversation, people who know you will speak well of you and others will want to meet you.

To build rapport when networking, give these behaviours a go:

- Act like you're the host of your own party.
- Aim to make others feel comfortable.
- Offer genuine smiles in which both the mouth and the eyes are engaged.
- Look at people directly.
- Lean towards the other person as they speak.
- Use open gestures, showing the palms of your hands.
- Keep your movements fluid and relaxed.
- Show interest by asking open questions.
- Keep your facial expressions warm and inviting.
- Find out what the other person needs.
- Offer to help however you can.

THE IMPORTANCE OF READING THE ROOM

Many years ago, when I was a new resident in a foreign land, I was invited to a party where I knew no one. Upon arrival, I couldn't find the hostess so ventured forth on my own. While the men looked a more interesting lot than the sensibly soled women, I knew that, as the new girl in town, introducing myself to the boys would not make the girls happy. Playing it safe – I thought – I approached a group of three worthy but dull-looking local matrons.

As I neared them, I noticed that they turned more inward towards themselves. Too late to stop and move in another direction, I extended my right hand in greeting and introduced myself by name. Barely flicking a glance in my direction over her shoulder, the group's spokesperson kept her hands at her sides and, with a downward turn of her mouth and eyes flickering over my person with disdain, said in a dull and lifeless tone, "Hello". She then turned back to her friends while I looked at my extended hand in wonder and surprise.

Not long afterwards, I ran a workshop at an industry conference where networking was the norm. Again, I was on my own. At the end of the day, during the cocktail hour, groups had formed by the time I arrived. Wanting to avoid a repeat of the previous story, I stood on the sidelines, watched, and waited. Soon, I spied a group of young professional women engrossed in lively discussion. One of the women spotted me. Her eyes were engaged and she was smiling a genuine smile. She gestured for me to join the group, which opened up and welcomed me into their conversation. Several weeks later, Kathrine invited me to speak at a conference her company was hosting. Years and many successful contracts later, she and I continue to enjoy working together, developing global communication skills programmes for her organization.

"The currency of real networking is not greed but generosity."

–Keith Ferrazzi

Sometimes you can get stuck in a going-nowhere conversation. The person is perfectly nice – just not someone you find particularly interesting. Rather than staying stuck, take control. Any one of the suggestions below will help you both move on to other conversations.

- *"Come join me while I top off my drink."* People tend to congregate near the bar, so you'll both be able to find others to talk with.
- *"I'm so enjoying our conversation and don't want to monopolize your time. Let's join the man/woman/group over there."* You may find that the person you're struggling to connect with engages easily with someone else.
- *"I have to speak with Amanda/Tony before they leave. Is there anyone you'd like me to introduce you to before I find them?"* Even if you don't know the person, you can walk up to them and say "John/Ann, I'd like to introduce you to George/Katrin" then leave them to get on with the rest while you find the person you wanted to meet.

The next time you attend a networking event, go with the following mindset.

1. It is better to give than to receive

Approach networking as an opportunity to build relationships. When you meet someone of interest, do offer them a favour or two before even considering asking them for something. The favour needn't be huge. Passing along an article you think they might find interesting or giving them the name of the maître d' at the hot new restaurant in town goes a long way in establishing valued and trustworthy relationships.

2. Have fun

Many people take the position that networking is a necessary evil, worse than the flu. If that's your attitude, change it now. Why would anyone want to engage with you if you approach people as though doing so is a drudgery? Let go of the concept of networking as a slog and see it as an opportunity to build solid relationships through the sharing of ideas and interests. You could do like some of my clients and approach networking events as a game; set up contests with other members of their teams who are attending to accomplish certain tasks.

3. Work your net

Social networking sites like Facebook and LinkedIn are great for business networking as long as you maintain contact with your contacts, or at least your top-tier connections. Pick up the phone. Arrange a face-to-face meeting. Networks will flounder and perish if you don't nurture them. By reaching out to others, you can create profitable and productive relationships for both of you.

4. Be curious
People who have a vast network of productive and profitable relationships are curious. Be it people, places, or things, these people are interested in what life has to offer. Open to opportunities and capable of tackling challenges, curious people are interesting to be with because they're interested in you. If you demonstrate a sincere interest in other people, they'll remember you in a positive way.

5. Cultivate your contacts
Ignore your contacts at your peril. Incommunicado for long periods of time and then you suddenly reach out, expecting an immediate response? Not the way to go. Touch base on a regular basis. Acknowledge important events in their lives. Birthday greetings, notes of congratulations, a handwritten thank you note – these go a long way in developing your network and strengthening rapport.

4

PERSUASION

.

"Not brute force but only persuasion and faith are the kings of this world."

Thomas Carlyle

Sandra wants Paul to do something for her. How can she convince him to comply?

1. Beat him with a bamboo branch.
2. Threaten him with a meal of crushed glass.
3. Establish rapport.

While beatings and threats may relieve your stress levels and make you feel all macho, and while these behaviours may work as persuasive techniques in the short run, they do little to promote trusting relationships. Openness, honesty, and integrity lie at the heart of persuading.

Before going any further, remember that this book is about non-verbal behaviour and the role it plays in various scenarios, including the process of persuasion. There are obviously many principles and techniques available out there about influencing and persuading in general, but this chapter specifically addresses the role of rapport, body language, and a bit about the voice. Just so we're clear.

RAPPORT IS YOUR PATH TO PERSUASION

What is rapport? Why is rapport important? How do you create rapport? What does rapport have to do with non-verbal behaviour? These are questions clients frequently ask.

Simply stated, rapport is a state of understanding feelings and communicating well. When you are in rapport with other people you accept and connect with them, treating one another with respect. When you're in a state of rapport you have a shared mental connection or bond. You "get" one another.

"I think there's a natural chemistry between us as friends; and there's really no separation between the rapport that we feel when we're in conversation and when we're playing music, it's one in the same."

–Benny Green

So why is rapport important? Because it's the gateway to success. When you want to persuade others, start by building a *trusting*, *ethical*, *respectful* relationship. That's rapport.

You create rapport by demonstrating interest in other people. You gain insight into their mental state by noting the following.

Facial Expressions

- **Eyes.** *The eyes are the mirror of the soul.* If another person avoids making eye contact with you, or tries to stare you down, give them the space to act out their negative behaviour before responding. You can say "I notice that..." or "Help me understand..." in order to get them to see things from your point of view. If their eyes are dull and lifeless, match their behaviour for a few minutes until they feel comfortable with you. Then you can change the mood by looking at them as you engage in conversation. If you've built a trusting relationship, the other person will return your gaze.

- **Mouth.** Pursed lips indicate a tight point of view as well as an unwillingness to communicate. A ready smile shows interest and welcomes you into the person's space. If someone seems disinclined to engage with you, smile and be patient. As long as you treat people with respect, they will eventually come around.

- **Face colour.** While you may find it difficult to mirror another person's blush, knowing how you feel when you go red helps you understand what the other person is experiencing. Demonstrating empathy is a pathway to persuasion.

Gestures

Observe the types of gestures and movements other people use if you want to understand their mindset. For example:

- Finger pointing at another person is a sign of aggression.
- A backward flick of the hand is a dismissive action.
- A jiggling foot indicates impatience.
- Rubbing the neck or throat is a signal that you need relief.
- Twined legs and clasped hands are signs of discomfort.

When seeking to persuade someone who's demonstrating negative behaviours, patience is required. You don't want to reflect back what you see, as doing so really lowers the tone of the interaction and reduces the chances of reaching an agreeable outcome.

Rhythm of Movement and Energy Levels

- If the other person's body is still and his gestures are few, you'll struggle to establish rapport if you're bouncing about in a Tigger-like fashion.
- Conversely, if the other person is full of energy and you're more contained in your actions, you'll find establishing rapport easier when you adapt your actions to match theirs.

Vocal Patterns

People's voices reflect their past and their present, their hopes and their fears. By identifying the sound, pitch, pace, tone, and volume of another person's voice you can tell whether they're feeling positive or negative. Knowing that guides you in choosing the best way to approach them.

- A resonant voice, like a church bell or a Tibetan monk's chime, is full, rich, and easy on the ear. People are drawn to resonant voices. This voice conveys authority and indicates power. Aim to match this sound when persuading them.

- A voice that is shoved in the nose, stuck in the throat, or buried in the depths of one's body indicates that the speaker is holding back something about himself. Ask them to tell you more about their thoughts and points of view to elicit useful information when the time comes to persuade them to see things another way.

- A voice that comes from high in the head is expressing excitement, enthusiasm, and energy. Adopt these tones to show that you're on the same wavelength.

- Slack muscles around the mouth and tight muscles around the jaw prevent clear articulation. Avoid these negative behaviours.

> 66 **People have deep and painful reasons for not wanting their voices to be heard. Respect that and encourage them to speak.** 99

Breathing Patterns

- Fast, slow, deep, or shallow, aim to match the other person's breathing rate and placement. This technique gives you an insight into what the other person is experiencing. A deep sigh is a sign of release. Quick, shallow breathing indicates anxiety.

- Avoid staying in a strenuous breathing pattern for too long. If you prolong taking short, shallow breaths too, you will start to feel anxious. Not a good feeling when you want to be persuasive.

Word Choice

The language people use and the way they deliver their message tells you about their point of view. When you know their mood and mindset, you're able to adapt your behaviour to communicate best with them.

- People who pepper their conversation with derogatory words and negative critiques tend to have low self-esteem and a pessimistic outlook. They struggle to establish and maintain eye contact. Their gestures are closed and include pointing fingers, clenched fists, tight lips, and a furrowed brow. They find establishing trusting relationships difficult. Other people avoid spending time with them because being in their company feels burdensome.

- People who include positive words and phrases when they speak are likely to have high self-esteem and view the world optimistically. They demonstrate interest in others. Their gestures are open and welcoming. They make eye contact, nod in agreement, and smile with understanding. Others are drawn to their company because of the positive energy they exude. Being in their company feels good.

- When you're looking to persuade someone to your point of view and their behaviour is positive, reflect back what you observe. When their behaviour is negative, listen, reflect, and address what you have noticed, using supportive language and behaviour, including:
  - nodding in acceptance and acknowledgement
  - leaning towards the other person
  - establishing and maintaining comfortable eye contact
  - smiling as appropriate
  - containing your movements and gestures
  - using phrases such as "I've noticed that…" "From what I've observed, you appear to be…" "What else can we do to…?"

- Demonstrating warmth, interest, and care goes a long way in getting others to come around to your way of thinking.

Posture

- A body that is limp and lifeless displays disinterest.
- A body that is upright and alert demonstrates engagement.

Reflect back the positive actions you notice. Acknowledge the feelings being displayed in the negative behaviour, by using supportive language and an even tone of voice.

When you establish rapport through mirroring and matching behaviours, your chances of persuading other people to see your point of view are increased.

 THE TALE OF THE TWO TRAINERS AND ME

One evening, after a long day at the office, I attended a workshop addressing rapport building. I was tired, the room was hot, and my energy levels were low. The trainer, whose name I can't recall, came bounding into the room like a basket of puppies. Every movement, every gesture was a tsunami of energy. I felt overwhelmed and disrespected. I recall no learning from the session.

Not long afterwards, I attended another workshop. This one was early in the morning. The journey to the venue was arduous. As in the previous workshop, I was tired, the room was hot, and my energy levels were low.

The difference between the two trainers was measurable. Based on clear observation, the second trainer matched my behaviour, including my energy levels. She sat down next to me, spoke quietly, and leaned towards me as we engaged. Her gestures were few and her movements were calm. Soon I felt comfortable in her company and she was able to persuade me to participate in the programme in ways I wouldn't have if she hadn't first gained my trust.

66 Persuading others to your point of view requires a trusting relationship, which can be created through establishing rapport. 99

You can establish rapport by mirroring and matching the behaviours you observe in a respectful way. By demonstrating similar actions, you're showing that you have comparable ways of addressing the world. You understand one another and are, as the Italians would say, *simpatico*, with a special bond between you.

One of my colleagues who loves to dance describes being in rapport as dancing with a partner whose body fits hers. They dance on the same wavelength, with firmness and flexibility. They move in sync and are comfortable and in tune with one another. There's a shared sense of peace and compatibility. She follows her partner because she trusts him.

She then goes on to say:

> *"Being out of rapport is like dancing with someone who is either rigid or flaccid. Neither is good. They either put no muscle into their movements or push and shove you around the dance floor with no sense of rhythm or harmony. **I don't feel compatible with them and don't trust them to guide me... dancing with them is no fun.**"*

People who get on well move in unison – leaning forwards, leaning backwards, making similar gestures at the same speed and rhythm. Applying these principles when you want to persuade others to your point of view is a vital part of the process.

66 With rapport, all things are possible. Without rapport, life is an arduous journey. 99

FOUR PRINCIPLES FOR BUILDING RAPPORT

1. Mirroring

When you mirror someone, you become the mirror image of them. For example, if you were standing in front of someone who raised her right hand with the palm facing towards you, you would raise your left hand with the palm facing towards her, creating a mirror image. Mirroring is not mimicking and should be subtle and respectful to avoid causing offence or embarrassment.

Mirroring should be subtle and respectful.

2. Matching

Imagine standing in front of someone who raises her right hand. Rather than raising your left hand, as you would if you were mirroring, raise your right hand too. Matching is different from mirroring in that it is less obvious and more outside your conscious awareness. When you're matching someone, allow a bit of time to pass between when the other person gestured and when you respond. Otherwise, you could come across as mocking and disrespectful, not good attitudes to display when you're trying to persuade someone to follow your lead.

Matching is less obvious and more outside your conscious awareness.

Mirroring and matching are ways of tuning into someone's thought processes and how they are experiencing the world. When you mirror and match you are listening with your whole body. When you are in rapport with someone this behaviour happens naturally, making you both more capable and more susceptible when persuading and being persuaded.

> 66 **Mirroring and matching others' actions doesn't mean repeating them exactly, movement for movement. Rather, you reflect the sense of what they're communicating.** 99

In addition to matching other people's movements, gestures, and expressions, you can mirror and match their voices.

The most persuasive voices are:

- **Relaxed.** The sound is free and resonant. The body is void of blockages caused by pressures and anxiety.

- **Approachable.** No judgements, prejudices, or sarcasm hamper your ability to connect. With a warm and inviting sound you encourage others to listen and respond.

- **Flexible.** Differing pitches, rhythms, and levels of intensity make for a persuasive voice. Engaging your listener, your persuasive voice opens the door to connecting with others and them responding in a positive way.

Before Stephen Covey came up with the idea, St Francis of Assisi spoke of seeking to understand before being understood. This brings us to the last two principles of building rapport. To persuade someone to see your point of view, seek to understand how they see their world first before taking them into yours. First pace, then lead.

3. Pacing

To persuade another person, pace them. This means listening attentively to that individual with the intention of understanding what's going on with them. This is where you aim to find common ground. *Pacing requires acknowledging a person, being patient with them, and giving them your full attention.*

- Pacing requires observation skills. Once you have listened to the words and vocal quality, noted the energy levels, seen the postures and gestures, AND absorbed all of this information, you adapt your behaviour and words to match the other person's in order to establish rapport.
- Pacing is sometimes equated to running alongside someone at the same speed. Pacing is also described as meeting other people where they are.

66 **Mirroring behaviours – not mimicking or mocking – creates a common bond.** 99

4. Leading

When you're leading, you've moved from pacing to guiding. You've established a trusting relationship by acknowledging and listening to another person and they are now prepared to follow your lead.

- Use open gestures, such as an upward-facing palm, a smile, or eye contact as a way of convincing others.
- Lean towards the other person as you speak to show you care about them.
- Use your arms and hands for pointing in the direction you want others to follow.

 PACING, LEADING, AND ACHIEVING YOUR GOAL

Andrew is an outstanding persuader of men and women based on his ability to establish rapport. I recently observed him serve as the Master of Ceremonies at an industry conference where he demonstrated a clear example of pacing and leading. He came onto the stage and said: "It's Tuesday morning, 8 am, the sun is shining outside while we're stuck in a dark conference hall. (Audience laughter) *You're all here because you accepted the invitation to come. You may be wondering what's going to happen over the next two days and I'm going to tell you, at some point.* (Audience laughter) *We're all here for the same reason: to connect with our colleagues, learn about our goals for the coming year, and celebrate our successes. I know you want to meet – if not exceed – your targets, and I know you're interested in learning how we're going to do that."*

Look at what Andrew said and how he delivered his message. He paced his listeners by meeting their reality: it was Tuesday morning, 8 am, the sun was shining, they were in a darkened conference hall, and they were there for the same reasons.

Once Andrew had paced the group, he then began leading them, indicating where he wanted them to go: "You may be wondering what's going to happen..." "I know you want to..." By pacing first he built rapport, enabling him to lead his listeners where he wanted them to go.

So, you've read about the impact of rapport on persuasion. I've told you how mirroring and matching other people's body language creates a bond of trust and comfortability. You accept – in theory – that pacing and leading takes people to where you want them to go. And you're willing to go along with the premise that people learn best by doing. Here's your chance to put the theory into practice.

1. Observe two people interacting. They can be your friends, family members, clients, colleagues, strangers in an airport lounge. The choice is yours. Note how they subconsciously mirror and match each other's non-verbal behaviours.

2. When you're in conversation with someone, consciously lean forward towards them. Keep your hands open and your arms and legs uncrossed. This open body language is intended to help you and the person you're talking to feel relaxed. If you notice that the other person has crossed his arms and legs, change your position to reflect his. After a while in this position, you can revert back to an open position. If the other person feels safe in your company, he will adopt a similar posture to yours.

3. When in conversation with someone, look at them approximately 60–85% of the time while they're speaking. You want them to feel recognized without making them feel uncomfortable. As well as making eye contact, nod in understanding, make encouraging sounds ("Um hm, I see, tell me more").

4. Smile.

5. Ask open questions. You'll find out more about the other person by asking questions that include the words "what", "where", "how", "who", and "when" than by asking questions that require no more than a "yes" or "no" answer.

6. Summarize what you hear. If any misunderstandings have occurred, here's where you can rectify them.

7. Find links for common experiences. Refer back to what the other person has said. Build on the other person's ideas.
8. Demonstrate empathy. Show that you can understand the other person's feelings and can see things from their point of view.
9. Let go of any judgements or preconceived ideas you may have towards the other person.
10. Admit when you've made a mistake. Being honest is the best tactic for building trust and establishing rapport.

5

ASSERTIVENESS

"There's boldness in being assertive, and there's strength and confidence."

Bryan Cranston

I f you remember nothing else from this chapter, remember this:

"You have the right to be assertive."

What this means is that you are entitled to express your feelings, needs, and ideas **in ways that don't violate others**.

Even if you don't see yourself as assertive, and struggle to act as if you are, by adopting the appropriate non-verbal behaviours you project the image of an assertive person. The more you're perceived as assertive, the more assertive you will feel. The more assertive you feel, the more you will behave as if you are. Before you know it, you will have become an assertive person.

Frequently, people struggle to act assertively because they're afraid of the consequences. For example, some fear being bullied, so they act in a **passive** way, while others fear being judged, so they come on in an **aggressive** manner. Still others behave in a passive aggressive way, for reasons too complex to explore here. Whichever way, they're not being **assertive**.

In this chapter I identify the differences between passive, aggressive, passive aggressive, and assertive behaviours and offer ways of responding to them. Once you're clear about the different styles and the impact each has on communication, you're better able to communicate clear, congruent messages.

When choosing how best to behave, remember that each communication style comes with its own set of benefits and costs. Even being assertive can carry a burden. For instance, if people have been accustomed to your behaving in a passive way, they may struggle to accept your assertive approach and try to undermine your efforts to change your style. Keep calm and carry on.

DEALING WITH PASSIVE BEHAVIOUR

"Passive pleasure is no pleasure at all."

–Arthur Adamov

When you behave passively, failing to express your honest feelings, thoughts, and beliefs, you are violating your own rights and allowing others to do so as well. Expressing your thoughts and feelings in an apologetic, self-effacing way gives others permission to disregard what you say.

People who behave in a passive way tend to think they don't count and that their beliefs, thoughts, and feelings are less important than those of others. They may worry that people will think badly of them or not like them, and that if they say "no" they will upset the other person and be held responsible for doing so.

All of that said, there's a payoff to being passive. Passive people are often praised for being selfless and good sports. They're rarely blamed if things go wrong because they've demonstrated no responsibility. Other people tend to take care of and look after their passive counterparts, who are then able to avoid, postpone, or hide from conflict, thereby reducing the threat of short-term anxiety.

On the downside, people who choose to behave in a passive way can explode in an aggressive manner when they're no longer able to suppress their pent-up stress and resentment. In addition, other people frequently make unreasonable demands of them and they often find themselves stuck in unhealthy relationships, and feeling a lack of self-esteem.

 KNOWING WHEN TO BACK OFF

Ted was throwing a tantrum. Nothing was going right, everything was wrong, and his staff were a bunch of idiots. Rather than pointing out to him that his choices had led to the current calamity and that he had a highly skilled and loyal team of individuals, everyone stayed silent while the rant continued. Once the air had cleared and several hours had passed, one of Ted's trusted team members spoke with him. He helped Ted see how he could have handled the situation in a less aggressive and more assertive way that didn't leave his staff short of breath and wondering why they bothered coming in to work that day.

When you want to avoid unpleasant situations, tension, conflict, and confrontation, behaving in a passive way is the recommended course of action. If, for example, your personal or emotional safety is under threat, you might want to keep your head down and your mouth shut until the storm has passed. While direct confrontation is sometimes the right choice, other situations require a more tempered approach.

You can spot passive behaviour through the following signs.

Facial Expressions

- **Eyes.** Averted gaze. Looking downwards.
- **Raised eyebrows** in anticipation. Winking when angry.
- **Mouth.** Trembling jaw and lip biting. Hint of a smile when being criticized or expressing annoyance. Laughing when angry.

Gestures

- **Posture.** Slouched, slumped, head down.
- **Arms and legs** crossed in protective position.
- **Self-comforting gestures** such as wringing hands, covering mouth, touching hair, stroking throat, finger fiddling.

If someone is demonstrating passive behaviour and you want them to open up and express what's on their minds, try the following:

- keep your expressions and gestures open
- thank and praise them for their contributions
- ask for their inputs
- smile and lean towards them when you speak
- look at them with a soft focus
- tilt your head when you listen
- maintain a calm demeanour
- listen to what they say and reflect back what you hear.

Maintain a calm and friendly demeanour if someone is demonstrating passive behaviour towards you.

Vocal Patterns

- **Tone.** Either over-soft or over-warm. Weak, unsteady, and quiet, often fading away. Frequently dull and monotonous or singsong and whining.

- **Word choice.** Apologetic ("I'm sorry to bother you"); self-denigrating ("This is probably a stupid point"); full of filler words ("Um, er, ah maybe, like, sort of"); frequent justifications ("I wouldn't normally ask/say anything").

- **Delivery.** Long, rambling, and filled with hesitant pauses.

- **Breathing pattern.** Short and shallow.

DEALING WITH AGGRESSIVE BEHAVIOUR

"Aggression is inherently destructive of relationships. People and ideologies are pitted against each other, believing that in order to survive, they must destroy the opposition."

–Margaret J. Wheatley

People who behave aggressively express themselves in inappropriate ways, violating the rights of others. Aggressive people frequently upset others as they put people down and keep them there in an effort to maintain superiority. When aggressive people feel threatened, they respond by attacking back.

People with aggressive tendencies view the world as a battle ground, with winners and losers, and put themselves in the first category. They are out for number 1 and approach people with the attitude of "I'll get you before you get me". They make others do their bidding and like the feeling of being powerful and in control. They see themselves as impervious and things tend to go their way.

Behaving aggressively comes at a cost. Aggressive behaviour creates enemies and builds resentment. People end up feeling fearful and paranoid. By always trying to control others, aggressive people struggle to relax. Their relationships are based on negative emotions and tend to be unstable. Because, at the heart of the matter, aggressive people tend to feel inferior, they compensate by putting others down. Underneath their bellicose behaviour are people who often feel shame, guilt, and a lack of self-esteem.

Signs that will tell you if someone is acting aggressively include the following.

Facial Expressions

- Tight facial expressions including sneering, scowling, and a firmly set jaw.

- Muscles around eyes and mouth are tense.
- Lips are pursed or in a thin line.
- Rolling eyes.
- Head tilted forwards.
- Skin hot and clammy.
- Eyes firmly fixed on the other person, looking down on them.

Gestures

- Intruding into the other person's space.
- Speaking to someone from over their shoulder.
- Staring down the other person.
- Turning away when someone else is speaking.
- Clenching fists and pointing fingers.
- Crossing arms.
- Striding about impatiently.
- Leaning over someone.
- Wrist flicking as a sign of dismissal.
- Pulling back.
- Short, shallow breathing.

Vocal Patterns

- Harsh, cold, strident, sarcastic, and condescending. Frequently shouts and tone rises into higher registers.
- Pace is fast, abrupt, and clipped. Fluent, with few hesitations.
- Word are often hostile, uncompromising, and belligerent.
- Emphasizes points by using blaming words ("It was your fault that...").

- Intimidating ("You'd better watch your step").

- Put downs ("How dumb can you be?").

- Bigoted language, including sexual and racist remarks.

- Opinions stated as facts ("That's a stupid idea").

- Boastfulness ("You're lucky to have me leading this team").

- Evaluative comments emphasizing concepts such as "should", "bad", and "ought".

- Threatening questions ("Who was the idiot who suggested that?").

When aggressive behaviour comes your way in the form of verbal and non-verbal messages as opposed to acts of physical violence, apply self-control. Breathe deeply and slowly. Keep your facial expressions still. Do not respond in a similar way, instead remain quiet to keep from escalating the situation. After the storm has passed you could tell the aggressor how their behaviour made you feel. If aggressive behaviour is a pattern, don't expect your feedback to change their behaviour.

If someone behaves aggressively towards you, do not respond in a similar way.

BULLIES DON'T ALWAYS WIN

A client was concerned about the behaviour of one of his senior leaders. Known for his aggression, including the use of denigrating language and threatening gestures, his team members were upset and unmotivated. Several had requested reassignments while others, fearful for their jobs, decided to hang in there, despite being disparaged and feeling disrespected.

Observing the leader in action was painful. During meetings he would interrupt and speak over others, even saying at one point "There's only room for one person to talk in this meeting, and that's yours truly" as he pointed to himself. His threatening language ("I'm warning you, if you don't do what I told you to do NOW, you won't be around much longer") and bullying behaviours, including jabbing fingers towards other people, slamming fists, and dismissive flicks of the wrist, were intimidating, menacing, and downright rude.

The worry was that the team leader could see nothing wrong in his behaviour. Referring to his team as being "made up of idiots", he believed that bullying others into submission produced better results than allowing individuals to take responsibility. Eventually, his attitude and behaviour cost him his job.

DEALING WITH PASSIVE AGGRESSIVE BEHAVIOUR

When you notice a disconnect between what a person says and what they do, you're looking at passive aggressive behaviour. Passive aggressive people tend to express their negative feelings in an indirect manner, rather than saying what they have to say upfront and out loud.

In addition, the passive aggressive person can be quite childlike, demonstrating an unwillingness to resolve any dispute. They can view the requests or demands of others as unfair or unjust, and instead of expressing their feelings, they bottle them up and harbour resentments.

At first, passive aggressive people may seem sincere and affable. They often appear to be complimentary. Only after you reflect on their words do you realize that the so-called compliment was actually masking a cheap jibe. They view everything as an attack on them and see life as unfair or unjust. They assume others know how they feel and believe that anything they don't approve of was intended to be an attack on them.

Passive aggressive people thrive on throwing the last punch. Even if an argument has been settled, they slip one last insulting remark into the conversation, allowing them to feel victorious. For a passive aggressive person, it is all about how the world impacts on them.

The following are signs to watch for.

Facial Expressions

- False smiles.
- Pursed lips.

- Sneering.
- Raised eyebrows in fake surprise.
- Widened eyes of innocence.
- Steely eyes of aggression.
- Avoiding eye contact.
- Laughing when angry.
- Smiling and winking when annoyed.
- Sulking.

Gestures

- Checking phones for messages or looking away when others are speaking.
- Crossed arms and legs.
- Body pulled back.
- Jerky, choppy gestures.
- Closed fists.
- Tense muscles.
- Finger pointing.

Vocal Patterns

- Sarcastic.
- Cold.
- Mumbling.
- Making wistful statements ("I wish I could…") instead of asking for what they want ("I'd like to…").
- Dropping hints.
- Small put-downs, insults, and back-handed compliments.

- Giving the other person the silent treatment when they don't respond to veiled requests.

- One-word answers.

- Asking threat-based questions, such as "Why would you think that's a good idea?"

- Saying expressions like "I'm fine" through gritted teeth.

Because passive aggressive behaviour is indirect and not always immediately recognizable, people find it particularly difficult to deal with. The following suggestions may help.

Pay attention to specific behaviours, including:

- Procrastination.

- Pretending not to see, hear, remember, or understand requests.

- Sulking and withdrawing.

- Gossiping.

- Excluding others.

- Undermining other people's efforts (like bringing someone cookies and ice cream when they're trying to lose weight).

- The silent treatment, including answering questions with one word.

By recognizing the signs, you are forewarned and can choose not to become entangled in a no-win power struggle. Give yourself silent messages like "He is being passive aggressive and I will not participate in his routine" or "I will not respond by yelling or being sarcastic because doing so will escalate the conflict".

Point out the elephant in the room. Because passive aggressive people avoid direct emotional expression and guard against open acknowledgement of their anger, identify it when it occurs. Your words should be factual and non-judgemental, such as "It seems to me that you're angry at me for bringing this up". Expect that once you've made your observations, the other person will deny that they're angry. In that case, verbally accept the defences for the time being, responding with something along the lines of "Okay, I just wanted to share that thought with you". Don't argue or point out the denial. By sharing your awareness of the other person's covert anger, you've sent a powerful message that you're aware of the game being played and that things need to change.

ADOPTING ASSERTIVE BEHAVIOUR

"There is a fine line between assertiveness and being relaxed."
–Justin Guarini

People who demonstrate assertiveness communicate their thoughts, feelings, and beliefs in an open, honest, direct manner without violating the rights of others. They feel good about themselves and are confident making their own decisions. They treat others, and themselves, with respect and hold the belief that all people bring value.

Assertive people won't allow others to take advantage of them and they won't attack you for being who you are. While they know that they may not always win their points, they are comfortable approaching whatever comes their way with a civil and courteous attitude.

The benefits of being assertive are many. For starters, when you stand up for yourself and act in a respectful manner towards others, your self-esteem rises. Your chances of getting what you want improve as you treat others with honesty and respect. Because assertive people can express themselves directly at the time, resentments don't build up. And, when you aren't feeling the need to protect yourself and are less self-conscious and preoccupied with your own needs, you're more able to engage with others in an easy and relaxed way.

Funnily enough, if you are moving from being passive or aggressive to becoming assertive, you may find the transition a bit painful. Family and friends who have benefitted from your previous style may try to sabotage your efforts. You may feel frightened as you reshape previously held beliefs and values. In addition, you may experience emotional discomfort, and you're guaranteed no outcomes. If so, remind yourself that the pain is worth the effort of becoming the person you're entitled to be.

 FLYING HIGH

Elly has been flying hot air balloons in Africa and Myanmar for over 20 years. She knows first-hand the importance of acting with assertiveness. Carrying a load of 16 passengers per basket, one hesitant move, unclear command, or display of arrogance could bring the basket crashing to earth, taking lives with it.

When Elly speaks, her voice is firm. Easy to hear, without her having to shout, Elly commands her space by using language that is respectful both to her crew and passengers. Her sentences are clearly articulated; she uses simple words and phrases, and focuses on the task at hand. Her gestures are few and sure, and while she refers to herself as Bossy Boots, those of us who have flown with her value her assertive behaviour and look to her as a role model.

When you communicate in the ways described as follows, you are being your assertive self at your best.

Facial Expressions

- Gentle, concerned, and determined to see things through.
- Direct eye contact without staring.
- Smiling when pleased.
- Frowning when angry.
- Calm demeanour.

Gestures

- Steady, smooth, and relaxed.
- Body upright and balanced.
- Feet firmly planted, slightly apart, to provide a stable base.
- Hand gestures open and used to emphasize points in a controlled way.
- Palms face upward in an inviting position, or downward when placating.

- Arms open, showing no threat or fear.
- Head nodding.
- Body leaning forward.
- Breathing deep and slow.

Vocal Patterns

- Firm and relaxed.
- Vocal tone mid-range, rich, and warm.
- Sincere, clear, and appropriately loud for the situation.
- Fluent with few hesitations and a steady, even pace.
- Words and expressions include:
  - "I" statements ("I want", "I like", "I don't like"), brief and to the point.
  - Cooperative phrases ("How would you approach this?" "How else could you do that?").
  - Definite statements of interest ("I would like to").
  - Suggestions phrased using inclusive language ("How about..." "What do you say..." "Would you like to...").
  - Constructive criticism without blame ("I feel annoyed when you interrupt me").
  - Seeking opinions from others ("How does that work with your plans?").
  - Openness to exploring other solutions ("How else can we solve this problem?").
  - Separating fact from opinion ("My experience is different").

To communicate in an assertive manner, make a conscious effort to apply the following principles:

1. Use the word "I" instead of "we" or "you" to control the conversation.
2. Practise good posture. Imagine that you're stretching from the crown of your head to the heels of your feet. Feel your shoulder blades meet at the middle of your back and picture them melting down your spinal cord as your chest expands and your neck lengthens, and your shoulders relax.
3. Use expressive gestures to support your points and clarify your meaning.
4. Speak clearly and practise pausing for emphasis.
5. Breathe deeply and slowly to demonstrate control.
6. Embrace the attitude that you are responsible for your feelings and actions.

6

MEETINGS

"Always go into meetings ... with a positive attitude.
Tell yourself you're going to make this the best deal
for all parties."

Natalie Massenet

Too often I hear clients complain that their time is being taken up with meaningless meetings, and they ask me:

"What would it take to make meetings more meaningful?"

A positive attitude, for starters.

So, how can you demonstrate a positive attitude and how can you get others to do the same?

In this chapter I look at the impact of attitudes on behaviours, and explore how vocal variety, facial expressions, and gestures influence the quality of your outcomes.

BEING AWARE OF YOUR ATTITUDES

Your moods, feelings, beliefs, and attitudes all impact on how you present yourself. Simply stated, positive attitudes reflect themselves in open facial expressions and gestures, while closed expressions and gestures indicate negative moods.

In most meetings, attitudes fluctuate. Interest, boredom, annoyance, and excitement are some of the emotions that you may notice. Along with the changes in attitude come changes in body language. The two most important attitudes for you to watch out for in meetings are *aggressive* and *conciliatory*.

Aggressive behaviours act as barriers to building rapport and inhibit productive communication. Behaviours include:

- tense bodies
- tight lips

- crossed arms
- finger pointing
- clenched fists
- furrowed brows
- lowered heads
- pulling away
- steely eyes
- rolling eyes
- speaking over others.

"Aggressive behaviour conveys hostile, argumentative, and destructive attitudes. "

When confronted with aggressive behaviour, back off. Matching angry gestures and words does no one any good and makes you look as bad as the other person. Give them time to calm down before interjecting. This may not happen immediately, so be patient. Better to say nothing in the heat of the moment than to confront an angry bear. Once the waters have calmed, you can respond. Leaning towards the other person, looking them in the eye and speaking in a calm, clear voice demonstrates power, authority, and confidence.

In addition, when you want to demonstrate strength, purpose, and determination in the face of aggressive behaviour, place your feet side by side and firmly underneath yourself to create a stable foundation.

Sit tall and straight with your feet firmly grounded to create a stable foundation.

If you want to make a point or close the discussion, purposefully shift in your seat, straighten you head, raise your hand with open fingers, palms facing front, and lean forward. To appear confident and in control, put one hand on your hip, and if you're seated, rest your other elbow on the surface in front of you while raising your hand in the "Stop" position. Lower your forehead, tighten your mouth, and look at the disruptive person from under raised eyebrows. Consider the situation before doing this. Your boss might not appreciate being handled this way.

Conciliatory behaviours act as conduits for building rapport and promote productive communication. Behaviours include:

- fluid body movements
- genuine smiles
- loose arms
- open palm gestures
- heads nodding in agreement/understanding
- engaged eye contact

- leaning forward
- tilting head
- listening for understanding
- letting others speak without interrupting.

66 Positive behaviour conveys attitudes that are constructive, affirmative, and interested. 99

 YOUR ATTITUDE DETERMINES YOUR OUTCOME

One of my clients is a politician. Our first assignment was to improve her non-verbal behaviours, particularly in meetings. Her goal was to demonstrate a caring and curious attitude, even if I don't care about the issue. Although she would lean forward when listening, tilting her head and nodding in understanding, her hands would clench as her right foot entwined itself around her left leg. Rather than smiling, her mouth would purse and her eyes would tighten, creating both a worried and an angry look. This tense and twisted posture made her feel restricted and appear guarded. She was viewed as being untrustworthy and insincere.

*When I asked her if she wanted to care or appear to care, she responded "I want to **appear** to care, because if I truly cared about every issue that crosses my desk, I'd drown in emotion and would achieve nothing. In order to make a meaningful difference, and achieve my goals, I pick my causes and appear to care about everything."*

With a clear goal in mind we addressed both her beliefs and behaviours. Having been taught to care about people less fortunate than herself, my client felt guilty for not caring about every issue that crossed her desk. Try as she might, non-verbal leakages would slip out, betraying her discomfort. When she finally gave herself permission to care according to her own values and not according to someone else's, her body language loosened up. For example, she no longer clenches her fists and fidgets with her fingers when stressed. Instead, she opens her palms and adopts the "Power Position" in which her elbows extend outwards and her fingertips touch at her waist. From this position, when she makes a strong point, her fingers point upwards. When making a conciliatory comment or listening with intent, her fingers point down.

Either direction, when she adopts the Power Position, she appears open, accessible, and in control.

In addition, rather than twisting her feet like a pretzel, she keeps them together, firmly placed beneath her. These changes reflect my client's attitude, which is compassionate, open, and firm. Her ratings have improved and she's perceived as genuine, trustworthy, and honest.

BEING AWARE OF YOUR BEHAVIOURS

Meetings are a fact of everyday life, whether they're informal conversations around the water cooler or the more formal variety behind closed doors.

Whatever the type of meeting, not all of the non-verbal messages you send and receive will be positive. Sometimes you have to adopt negative behaviours to let others know that you're neither pleased nor impressed. At other times you may have to keep your mouth shut while others are on the attack. When you're aware of what non-verbal behaviours convey, you can pick and choose which ones to display according to the situation and your desired outcomes.

Because the face is the best indicator of emotional states, pay special attention to movements around the eyes, mouth, and nostrils as well as to breathing patterns and changes in skin colour. Brief, involuntary facial expressions that flash across a person's face display concealed emotions. Pay close attention to a person's face to spot suppressed feelings. *Be advised:* an adept observer can spot your emotions through the same channel.

Disgust	Anger
• Upper and lower lips raised • Nose wrinkled • Cheeks raised • Lines show below the lower eyelid	• Eyebrows lowered and drawn together • Vertical lines appear between the brows • Lower lid tensed • Eyes stare hard or bulge • Lips can be pressed firmly together with corners down or square shape as if shouting • Nostrils may be flared • The lower jaw juts out
Fear	**Contempt**
• Brows raised and drawn together, usually in a flat line • Wrinkles in the centre forehead between the brows, not across • Upper eyelid raised, but lower lid tense and drawn up • Upper eye has white showing, but not the lower white • Mouth open and lips slightly tensed or stretched and drawn back	• Asymmetrical smile, one side of mouth lifted • Eyes rolling

(Continued)

(Continued)

Happiness	Sadness
• Corners of the lips drawn back and up • Lips may or may not be parted, teeth exposed • A wrinkle runs from outer nose to outer lip • Cheeks raised • Outer corners of the eyes lifted • Crows' feet near the outside of the eyes	• Inner corners of the eyebrows drawn in and then up • Skin below the eyebrows triangulated, with inner corner up • Corner of the lips drawn down • Jaw comes up • Lower lip pouts out
Surprise	
• Brows raised and curved • Skin below the brow stretched • Horizontal wrinkles across the forehead • Eyelids opened, white of the eye showing above and below • Jaw drops open and teeth are parted, but there is no tension or stretching of the mouth	

The following charts contain further examples of positive and negative behaviours.

Facial Expressions

Negative	Positive
• Frowning • Avoiding eye contact • Staring • Tense jaw • Tight lips • Sneering • Chewing on lips • Skin texture: moist and flushed	• Smiling • Loose jaw • Engaged eye contact • Skin texture: cool and dry

Gestures

Negative	Positive
• Shrugging shoulders	• Arms held slightly away from body
• Crossed arms	• Open hands
• Clenched fists	• Palms visible
• Finger pointing	• Precise
• Fist slamming	• Contained
• Head thrusts	• Facing the speaker
• Lowered forehead	• Head tilts
• Flared nostrils	• Head nods
• Leaning back	• Leaning forward
• Turning away from the speaker	• Erect posture
• Erratic or lethargic movements	• Shoulders back and down
• Slumped posture	• Chin slightly lifted
• Body unbalanced	• Body balanced
	• Smooth
	• Fluid
	• Purposeful

Vocal Patterns

Negative	Positive
• Monotone	• Varied
• Dull, lifeless	• Resonant
• Mumbling	• Firm
• Harsh	• Deep and mid-level tones
• Grating	• Comfortable with silence
• Shouting	• Appropriate volume
• Inappropriate volume (too loud, too soft)	• Evenly paced
Breathing Patterns	
• Short	• Slow
• Shallow	• Deep

A simple technique for spotting attitudes is to observe the behaviour. Facial expressions, head positions, movements, and gestures reveal the thoughts and feelings that lie within. In simple terms, open behaviours indicate a positive mindset, while closed behaviours convey negativity.

SPOTTING DISINTEREST IN MEETINGS

In this 24/7 connected world in which we work, meetings can be a major annoyance – requiring time, patience, and attention. When meetings go on for too long, are poorly structured, and seem irrelevant, people can get bored.

Signs that indicate boredom, distraction, or plain old frustration include:

- **Fixated eyes and an unwavering head.** Genuine interest consists of a back-and-forth interchange, including anticipatory nods and eye contact passing amongst the participants. Dull eyes and little animation indicate lack of engagement.
- **Forced smiles.** Too long, too bright, and too fixed; smiles in which the eyes remain unengaged signal ennui.
- **Jiggling feet, tapping fingers, checking the smartphone.** Unconscious signals leak from the body.
- **Doodling.** While doodling can be a sign of boredom or impatience, some people doodle as a way of following the discussion.

If you notice these behaviours, suggest taking a break. Changing the mood by giving everyone the chance to stretch their muscles and shake out stiff limbs can lift the tone of the meeting and put it onto a productive track.

Seating Matters

Studies into the dynamics of seating arrangements demonstrate that the type of table and people's positions around it are vital elements in determining the effectiveness of meetings. Where you sit reflects your status and impacts how others perceive you.

If you're feeling adaptable and want people to feel comfortable, let them choose where to sit. Welcome them into the meeting, by gesturing with an open palm, tilting your head towards the table, offering a genuine smile and flashing your brows as you do so. These gestures are warm and inviting and promote a relaxed atmosphere.

If the meeting is going to be a tough one, position the people yourself. Indicate the place where you want them to sit with a pointed finger and a turned-down hand. This gesture is directive, commanding, and demonstrates control.

Pointing with a turned-down hand is commanding and demonstrates control.

DEMONSTRATING NEGATIVE POWER

I once attended a meeting where the leader never sat down. He created a barrier between himself and the rest of the group by standing behind both the table and the chair. As he spoke, walking around the room, he forced the rest of us to shift in our seats in order to focus on him, demonstrating aggressive behaviour that put the rest of us at a disadvantage.

Suggested Seating Positions For Specific Purposes

- Positioning your body at a 45-degree angle encourages relaxed, friendly conversation and **open discussion**.

- If you want to **exert influence** over someone, sit directly across from them. From here you can establish direct eye contact and easily observe their body language.

- Sitting side by side fosters **cooperation**.

- If you want others in the meeting to **notice you**, sit to the right of the person in power. When people look at this person they see you too, and their subconscious associates you with influence and authority.

- **For problem-solving**: encourage high levels of interaction and participation by seating participants at a round table where everyone has an unobstructed view of the others. In this arrangement, reflective of King Arthur and the Knights of the Round Table, there is no head. Everyone is considered equal. Participation and open discussion are encouraged.

Be advised: while King Arthur's Round Table promotes equality, who sits where in relation to the *perceived leader* still denotes positions of status and power. The people sitting on either side of the person with the highest status – and, therefore, power – hold the next level of influence, the individual sitting on the right being granted more clout than the individual sitting on the left. Power lessens the farther away from the high-status individual a person sits. Whoever sits directly across from the person with the highest status is placed in a competitive position.

- If your meeting is for **training** purposes, choose a U-shaped table. This arrangement allows presenters and participants to see and interact with one another easily. The delegates are accessible and the presenters can choose to move in and out of the space, depending on how close and comfortable they want to be with the group.
- For **decision-making**, place the leader at the head of a rectangular table. In **hierarchical seating arrangements**, attendees sit in order of descending authority, with the meeting chairperson sitting at the head.
- For the **best discussions**, seat people with opposing viewpoints opposite each other. Avoid putting **conflicting personalities** next to or across from one another. Sprinkle them throughout the group.

“**When attending meetings, take note of the type of seating arrangement and who sits where in order to understand the dynamics in the room.**”

Determining Status

A chair's height is associated with status and power: the higher you are, the more authority you hold. Savvy business types know that by adjusting the seat height of their chairs, they gain a competitive advantage as they look down on others in the meeting.

Chairs with a high back, arm rests, and that are on casters convey more power than a fixed chair with no arms and a low back.

If you're offered a chair that puts you at eye level with the desk in front of you, politely decline, saying that you prefer to stand. You don't want to look like a child in kindergarten. Aim to sit at the same level as the person running the meeting to establish equality. Placing yourself in a lower position automatically indicates your lack of power and status.

Meetings offer you the opportunity to display behaviours that can advance your career. You can also torpedo your job opportunities through negative, disruptive behaviours. Demonstrating patience, acknowledgement, and a willingness to listen will move you up the ladder as opposed to behaviours that demonstrate negativity. The choice is yours.

Practise different postures and facial expressions while observing yourself in the mirror. Even better, get someone to video you (or video yourself) as you adopt the different positions and poses.

The purpose is for you to experience the sensations associated with different facial expressions, gestures, and body movements, and the impact they have in meetings.

To further understand how your body language impacts on the way you communicate, watch Amy Cuddy's TED talk. https://www.ted.com/speakers/amy_cuddy

7

INTERVIEWS

"When you're interviewing someone, you're in control. When you're being interviewed, you think you're in control, but you're not."

Barbara Walters

Today's the day. Having landed an interview for your dream job you're about to be put through your paces. You're excited, anxious, energized, and nervous. You want this job badly, as do several other contenders. In order to win this role, you have to look, act, and sound like the perfect person for the part.

So, what do you do about your sweating palms, your dry mouth, and the butterflies in your stomach? How do you keep your fingers from fidgeting and your feet from jiggling? How do you keep from tugging at your collar or picking at your cuticles? While these symptoms are all normal responses to stress, none of them represents you at your best.

The choices you make – including, but not limited to:

- how you dress
- your personal grooming habits, and
- the way you behave

all demonstrate your suitability for the position. They send signals about how you perceive yourself and influence how others view and respond to you. As always, the choices you make inform the interviewer's decisions about whether you're right for the role or not.

"Knowledge is power."

–*Francis Bacon*

Preparing For Your Interview

Begin preparing for your interview by *researching the organization*. The more you know, the better prepared you are to give thorough, informed answers to the questions.

- What is the organizational culture?
- What are the values?
- How are your culture and values similar to/different from theirs?
- How can you demonstrate that you and the organization are aligned?

What Do You Know About Your Interviewers?

Find out as much about them as you can. Check out Facebook, LinkedIn, Twitter, and any other social media sites you can find. If you know someone who knows the individual, either personally or professionally, ask questions. For example:

- Where did they study (schools, universities, advanced degrees)?
- What organizations are they members of?
- What are their interests and hobbies?
- What is their marital and family status?

"You can learn a lot about a person by paying attention to what you observe."

Find out what issues they're currently facing. Position yourself as the person who can ease their pain. The more information you have going into the interview, the better prepared you are for nailing the job.

- Show interest in their needs,
- curiosity about their concerns, and
- demonstrate your ability to solve their problems.

"I want guys who want to be here. I want guys who are energetic and passionate. I didn't see any passion from Todd. You could tell from his body language that he didn't want to be here."

–Perry Florio

Having done your research, now's the time to focus on yourself.

Going Into the Interview

From the moment you enter the building, adopt the behaviours of a person who's keen, willing, and able. Set yourself up for success by putting a spring in your step and a smile on your face. Remind yourself of your strengths and what you bring to the job, then demonstrate that in the way you move. You never know who might be standing next to you in the elevator, or following you down the hall. Powerful, influential people have a habit of observing from afar and popping up at unexpected times and in unexpected places.

Your body language can have a great impact on how you're perceived, right from the moment you enter the building.

When you reach reception, introduce yourself and state whom you're there to see. Focus your attention on the person to whom you are speaking. Establish eye contact. Smile. Enunciate clearly, speaking just loudly enough for the receptionist to hear you without blasting out the lobby. State your name with pride and pleasure. Speak slowly, enabling the other person to catch your words.

When you are taken into the interview room, remain standing until you're invited to sit. For the duration of the interview, adopt the behaviours that assure your interviewers both that you want to be there and that you're the person for the job.

If the interview is taking place in the interviewer's office, look around. Do you notice family photos? Collectable art work? Awards and citations? Is the interviewer's desk in order or are papers scattered about? The state of a person's personal space tells you about what's important to them, which then informs how they behave.

66 When interviewing, engagement is key. 99

Follow the suggestions below to ensure that you create a positive first impression.

Facial Expressions
- Smooth forehead.
- Comfortable eye contact, not staring.

- Eyes slightly widened.
- Sides of mouth and eyes lifted in a smile.
- Relaxed jaw.
- Skin cool and dry.

Gestures

- Head held horizontally.
- Chin lifted.
- Firm hand shake, matching pressure of the other person's.
- *A word of warning:* avoid shaking hands with your palm facing down as that action can be perceived as arrogant. As for the double-handed handshake – in which you put your left hand on top of the other person's hand – don't even think about it.
- Lean forward to show interest and enthusiasm.
- Hands calm and visible. Take notes to give them something to do if you think they might fidget.
- Specific gestures, kept to a minimum.
- Arms uncrossed, slightly extended from your sides to fill your space.
- Nodding to show understanding and agreement.
- Move with purpose, focus, and controlled energy.
- Hand gestures kept between mid-chest and waist level.

Vocal Patterns

- Speak slowly. When you're nervous, the tendency is to speak quickly.
- Enunciate clearly.
- Pronounce names properly.
- Speak at an appropriate volume for the space.
- Use positive, compelling language to engage your listener.
- Pause before answering questions to demonstrate thought and maturity.
- Make your points clearly and concisely.
- Breathe deeply and slowly to calm your nerves.

In addition, **dress appropriately**. For example, if you're interviewing for a job at a law firm or an investment bank, pick a conservative suit. If you're interviewing for a position at start-up or in the arts, you can be more casual in your attire. And please, make sure that you're well groomed. Chewed, dirty fingernails, frayed collars, bad breath, and unkempt hair are revolting.

Finally, **when the interviewers stand up, mirror their behaviour by standing up too**. Look them in the eye, wait to be offered before shaking their hands, smile, and thank them for their consideration. Just before you leave the room, pause slightly at the door, turn back to look at your evaluators, and give them a final smile. Step back out of the door so that the last image they have of you is your engaged face, not your backside.

Should self-doubt seep into your psyche at any point during the interview process, turn off the tap and focus on the task at hand. Assume the actions of your most confident self as described above, and bingo! While I can't promise you'll land the contract, I do promise that you'll impress the punters and will feel good about yourself in the process.

Before going into an interview, visit the restroom. Check yourself in the mirror to make sure you're looking shipshape. Then smile, lift your head high, widen your stance, and stretch your arms upwards and outwards.

Ideally, you would hold that position for two minutes to get your hormones pumping and set you up for an engaging interview.

This position of power (think Superman and Superwoman) gets the testosterone flowing, eliciting a commanding presence.

Before leaving the room, shake out your hands, arms, and legs, look in the mirror, and give yourself another big smile.

Today just might be your lucky day.

8

NEGOTIATION

"Let us never negotiate out of fear. But let us never fear to negotiate."

John F. Kennedy

Negotiation is a fact of life and everything in life is negotiable. Although some people seem to negotiate naturally, negotiation skills are learned skills, not inherited traits. As with learning any new skill, practice, patience, and perseverance are required.

From the boardroom to the bar, people need to back up their words with non-verbal behaviours that radiate **openness, honesty, and confidence**. Those actions put into play – backed up by an **optimistic attitude** – foster trust. Others are then prepared to cooperate and together you reach a mutually satisfying agreement.

Because the way people behave is a sure indicator of their frame of mind, point of view, and general sense of well-being, pay attention to their physical signs and signals to gauge their true attitudes and intentions.

When preparing to enter into a negotiation, learn as much as you can about the other people involved. Culture, beliefs, experiences, and values all impact on how people behave and approach the negotiation process.

 WORDS FROM MY FATHER

When I first started in business, I turned to my father for advice on how to get the best deals from my suppliers and clients. Dad said, "Negotiation is about knowing what you want, going after it, and respecting the other person in the process." He told me that compromise is the name of the game and that I should look after myself and be willing to budge in

> *order that everyone feels satisfied. Over the years I am*
> *consistently reminded that negotiation is about building*
> *relationships rather than burning bridges.*

Before going into the details of non-verbal behaviour in negotiations, consider the following suggestions.

1. **Show up on time.** In order to get the negotiations off on the right foot, make sure that you arrive on time. As Woody Allen puts it, "*Eighty percent* of success is sh*owing up.*" Before someone opens their mouth or offers their hand in welcome, the way they treat time indicates how they might treat you. Showing up late for a negotiation damages the process in two ways. Firstly, the **latecomer** is perceived as **discourteous,** if not outright **insulting**. In addition, a lack of punctuality implies **incompetence** and **lack of integrity**. Other people feel irritated and less inclined to make a deal.

Secondly, the late arrival ends up feeling **stressed, distracted and insecure** as opposed to the state of calm, focused, and confident that they want to experience as they enter into the negotiation process. Different cultures have different attitudes towards time, and may arrive late for the meeting. Don't let that upset you. Remain calm and focus on the task.

2. **Shake hands.** While the days of sealing a deal with a firm handshake may well be gone, shaking hands promotes trust. A firm handshake that matches the pressure of the other person's hand is ideal. Both your hand and the other person's connect palm to palm, with the web between your thumb and forefinger meeting in an upright position. While you may wonder about the person who offers you a limp fish or a bone-crusher handshake, research shows that all handshakes put people at ease, display integrity, and increase cooperative behaviours.

Be aware: if someone turns their wrist over, putting their palm horizontal to the floor and making the other person's palm face up, you're witnessing a power play.

3. **Identify baseline behaviours.** Before a negotiation begins, you usually have a chance to interact with the people from the other side of the table when they're not under pressure. The way a person behaves while enjoying a croissant and coffee during the meet and greet may be different from the way they behave when the atmosphere is laced with stress and tension. Pre-negotiation, observe how the other people behave. Ask them questions, to which you already know the answers. Observe how the individuals react as they answer. If they're being honest, you'll notice calm and relaxed movements and facial expressions. If they're not being honest, you'll spot the give-away behaviours, such as jerky gestures, averting their eyes or staring you down, shuffling feet, and tense facial expressions. Once negotiations begin, you have a base of behaviours from which to judge the other person's levels of honesty.

"During a negotiation, it would be wise not to take anything personally. If you leave personalities out of it, you will be able to see opportunities more objectively."

–Brian Koslow

Facial Expressions

Breathing patterns, movements of the mouth, eyes, and jaw, even the temperature of someone's skin signals a person's thoughts, emotions, and intentions. Note the following signs to detect a person's state of mind throughout the negotiations. These expressions will come and go according to how the individual is feeling at the time.

Negative Facial Expressions

- Frowning.
- Flaring nostrils.
- Tense lips.
- Sides of the mouth turn downward.
- Tight jaw.
- Staring intently.
- Avoiding eye contact.
- Flushed colour.
- Perspiring.
- Chin pulled inward.
- Chin thrust upward.

Negative behaviours indicate a closed mind, recalcitrance, and disinterest. If you see these behaviours during a negotiation, nod your head in acceptance, lean towards the person, and keep your face calm and your gestures controlled. Use respectful language as you seek a common ground. Reflecting back negative behaviours and words ensures a lose–lose result.

Positive Facial Expressions

- Smooth forehead.
- Cool, dry skin tone.
- Comfortable eye contact, steady gaze, soft focus.
- Calm mouth, corners slightly lifted.
- Soft jaw.
- Smiling.
- Nodding head in agreement.
- Chin horizontal or slightly lifted.

Positive expressions indicate openness, willingness, and interest. When you observe these signs, you're in luck. Reflect back what you notice, mirroring and matching the other person's words, facial expressions, and gestures to cement rapport. (For more about establishing rapport, see Chapter 3.)

Gestures

Anxiety and other negative emotions can leak out of a person's body before they have time to stop the flow. Watch for the following movements and gestures to detect **nervousness, anxiety, and stress**:

- short, shallow breaths
- lowered head
- fiddling fingers, clenched fists, entwined hands
- self-touching
- pulling back
- crossing and uncrossing arms and legs
- tapping feet.

When you encounter these behaviours, resist the urge to judge or assume, and try to be objective. Rather than taking them as a personal attack on you, see them as nothing more than the other person's state of mind. Avoid mirroring similar gestures and movements. Lean forward, with open gestures and facial expressions. Address what you observe using language such as: "You seem to be feeling doubtful about this…" "What are your concerns…" "Help me to understand…" By acknowledging what you notice in a non-threatening way, you stand a chance of turning the tide.

Behaviours that indicate a **calm and thoughtful mindset** include:

- deep and slow breathing pattern
- hands still, visible, and at waist height
- arm and hand gestures open
- specific hand gestures to illustrate or support points
- sitting or leaning forward
- head nodding as a sign of acknowledgement and acceptance
- feet in a steady position.

When you see these gestures, you can bet that you're onto a winner. Mirror back what you notice to build rapport and reach a mutually satisfying outcome.

Here are some other behaviours to watch out for in the negotiating room and what they mean:

- Unbuttoning a jacket or rolling up sleeves says "I'm relaxed, ready to get down to business".

- Fast blinking indicates alertness, lying, or discomfort.
- Tilted head with knuckles under chin indicates interest.
- Resting chin in heel of hand suggests boredom.
- Ear tugging signals that the listener wants to hear more.
- Scratching the head is a sign that someone is uncomfortable with the discussion.
- Steepling of fingers denotes confidence.
- Hand on back of neck, or finger under collar, shows annoyance.
- Fiddling with a pen is a sign of needing more time.
- Object in mouth signals a need for reassurance.
- Taking off eyeglasses and setting them down indicates the person is shutting you off.

A tilted head with the knuckles under the chin can indicate interest.

Vocal Patterns

In the heat of the moment, the stress of the negotiation combined with a person's passion to make their point can cause them to raise their voices, rush their words, or interrupt others. When negotiating:

- listen without interrupting
- pause to show thought
- respond slowly and in calm tones
- speak in a respectful manner.

A point about pausing: pausing before responding can tap into a person's insecurities. Some people believe they have to fill the air with the sound of their voice and are uncomfortable with silence. Other people feel insecure when the speaker stays silent, afraid that they might be challenged. Remaining silent is a great way to get others to talk. As Lance Murrow advised:

> *"Never forget the power of silence, that massively disconcerting pause which goes on and on and may at last induce an opponent to babble and backtrack nervously."*

In addition to paying attention to non-verbal behaviours, take note of the language that is used to get a feel for the emotional temperature and levels of integrity in the room. For example:

- Statements that mean just the opposite ("In my humble opinion...").
- Off-the-cuff comments preceding major announcements ("By the way", "As you are aware").

- Legitimizers ("Honestly", "Frankly").
- Justifiers ("I'll try").
- Erasers ("But", "However").
- Deceptions ("I'm not very smart when it comes to...").
- Preparers ("I don't mean to impose, but...").
- Exaggerators ("This is very embarrassing...").
- Trial balloons ("Off the top of my head...").

When you know what emotions others are experiencing, you can adjust your behaviour to either cool them down or spur them on. The most important thing for you to remember is to keep your head when others are on the verge of losing theirs.

Seating Positions

Where someone sits at the negotiation table indicates the status of that person. The most powerful person in the room will either sit at one end of the table or the other, or will take the middle seat along the length of the table. Next to the person with power sit the trusted advisors and supporters.

In addition, where people sit influences how they manage the negotiations. For example:

- When you're negotiating with two people, sit where you can watch both.
- When two people are on your team, sit apart so you "speak with two different voices".
- When your large group opposes their small group, keep your group together for power.
- When their large group opposes your small group, intermingle to diffuse their power.

NEGOTIATE WITH THE RIGHT PEOPLE

As my late brother, a former Army officer, successful business man, and avid poker player once advised me: "You have to know which table to sit at and you have to be prepared to change tables." His message was: Negotiating is about doing the deal in a smart way that produces the best results.

When you are not happy with the way a negotiation is going, silently count to ten. This gentle, soft indication of your disapproval usually elicits a response from the other party as the natural tendency is to fill silence with sound. Once they start talking, you have a better idea of what they have to offer.

If you struggle to remain silent, push your tongue to the top of your mouth while keeping your lips shut. From that position your facial expression remains still and your mouth can't open.

9

SALES

"I like to think of sales as the ability to gracefully persuade, not manipulate, a person or persons into a win-win situation."

Bo Bennett

f you think sales is an easy sleazy business, think again. Sales is about making friends, investing in relationships, and getting others to see the world the way you do. Sales is about sharing your passion, convincing individuals to believe and buy into your concept, product, and services. Sales challenges even the toughest competitors, as it demands the discipline to persevere and prove your worth. Sales rocks.

In this chapter we look at the attitudes and behaviours that impact on the sales process, which at its core is all about building relationships and delivering on promises.

> "Sales are contingent upon the attitude of the salesman – not the attitude of the prospect."
>
> *–W. Clement Stone*

PICKING YOUR ATTITUDE

To quote Henry Ford, "Whether you think you can or think you can't, you're right." Attitude determines your future. When the market is crashing, jobs are scarce and sales are hard to make, maintaining a positive outlook is tough. Get over it. Rather than wallowing in a "woe is me" state of mind, pick yourself up, dust yourself off, and start all over again. What's another cold call when you've already made 200? Who knows, this time you might be lucky.

To help you develop a positive attitude, behave in a positive way. The following tips will get you started.

- **Stand up straight. Sit up tall. Expand your chest. Raise your chin.** Slouching and slumping lowers your energy levels, making you feel and appear uninspired and disengaged. Lean slightly forward, allowing your chest to expand and your shoulders to roll back gently and down.

- **Engage your eyes.** As opposed to a dull gaze, which denotes boredom, bright eyes show interest. Eyes that are softly focused demonstrate care and concern. Be careful not to over-connect, as staring is odd and creepy.
- **Smile.** Let the muscles at the outer corners of your mouth and eyes lift, creating a welcoming expression. Lifting the lips is not enough. If the eyes are not engaged in the act, the smile will look forced and fake.

By taking on the behaviours of someone who's up for the chase, you will find yourself believing that you can convince even the toughest client. And once you believe that you can, you can.

 TAKING A DIFFERENT PERSPECTIVE

Times were tough, sales were down, and Bob was worried. He complained to his sales manager that the economy was terrible, no one was buying, his customers hated him, and that he couldn't get past the gatekeeper at his biggest opportunity. His dejected body language, hangdog expression, uninspiring vocal quality – an irritating combination of whiney and lifeless – and negative choice of words showed that he was ready to throw in the towel.

Earlier in the day, Jane had gone into the sales manager's office with a different attitude and set of

> *behaviours. She was pumped. Even though she was struggling to hit her quotas for the month and had only 10 days to go, her eyes were sparkling, her face was glowing, her voice was lively, her words were positive, and she had a big smile on her face. Her boss was impressed with her confident attitude, which she displayed in her upbeat body language, convincing words, and animated voice.*

Sales can be a desperate business, leaving you chewing your nails, biting your lips, and tearing your hair out. Sales can also be rollicking good fun for those who enjoy the thrust and parry of the commercial world. How you perceive doing deals and how you behave in the process determine if you will take home the bacon or show up empty handed.

BUILDING RELATIONSHIPS

"Pretend that every single person you meet has a sign around his or her neck that says, 'Make me feel important.' Not only will you succeed in sales, you will succeed in life."

–Mary Kay Ash

People like people who make them feel important. People like doing business with people who make them feel important. People like hanging out with people who make them feel important. The message? Make people feel important.

Tips for making people feel significant, essential, and like they matter include:

- **Looking at them when they speak.** When you look at someone while they're sharing their thoughts, ideas, and feelings, they feel acknowledged. Be sure to keep your gaze open and soft, not scowling or staring.
- **Nodding in affirmation, understanding, and interest.** Demonstrate that you're receptive, interested, and able to empathize.
- **Leaning forwards to get closer to the other person.** While you don't want to invade anyone's territory, moving closer to a person demonstrates that you find them interesting and want to know them.
- **Using open gestures.** Gesturing when engaging keeps the conversation alive and vibrant. Using open palm gestures shows the other person that you're non-threatening and can be trusted. Making people feel safe makes them feel that they matter.

DEMONSTRATING CONFIDENCE

People like doing business with people they know they can count on. Customers, clients, and even your colleagues want to know they can trust you. Your posture, your facial expressions, the way you position your feet all tell whether you're the real deal or just a fake. The following is a table of behaviours that demonstrate confidence, credibility, and a compelling personality.

Behaviours which demonstrate confidence, credibility and a compelling personality

Vocal Quality	Facial Expressions	Movements	Gestures	Word Choice
• Low and mid-level tones • Resonant, rich, and warm • Appropriate volume • Clear articulation • Comfortable pausing • Slow, deep breathing	• Muscles pull up and outwards • Face is calm • Forehead is smooth • Cheeks are lifted • Engaged eye contact • Outer corners of eyes turn up • Outer sides of mouth lift • Cool, dry skin	• Measured • Considered • Precise • Firm • Deliberate • Controlled	• Open hands • Palms face forward and upward • Hand chops with closed fingers • Hands gently pulsating forward or downward (stop position) • Upright posture • Hand gestures kept between waist and mid-chest level • Upward or downward-facing Power Position (elbows bent, fingertips meet at waist level) • Arms slightly extended from body • Body weight evenly distributed	• Specific • Precise • Positive phrasing • Respectful • No fillers (um, er, ah) • No qualifiers (sort of, kind of, like) • No excuses

SHOWING INTEREST

If you want to make current customers and potential clients feel that you care about them and want to ease their pain, demonstrate the following behaviours:

- **Mirror their speech patterns.** Speak at the same speed and with the same tone as others. If you speak too fast, the other person might feel pressured. If you speak too slowly, they might think you are lazy or speaking down to them.

- **Make eye contact and avoid staring.** Too little contact and you appear insecure or disinterested. Too much feels a bit strange. Aim for 65–85% of your listening time to be spent having direct eye contact. When you're speaking, a target of 45–75% is good.

- **Tilt and nod your head when listening.** A simple way to show that you're attentive and caring is to slightly tilt your head to either side and slowly nod.

- **Lean towards the person.** Both when you're listening and speaking, incline your body in the direction of the other person to demonstrate closeness, empathy, and commonality.

- **Remain calm.** Holding your hands upwards and rubbing them vigorously demonstrates excitement. Clenching them together signals frustration. Keep your hands in front of you or by your sides, in a relaxed position, with your fingers together and slightly curved open.

Aim to behave in a gracious, honest, and generous way. Mirroring the other person's movements and expressions, and using open gestures, signals that you're approachable and receptive. As one of my clients says, "Sales is all about consistently demonstrating to the customer that you care about them and their needs."

You may notice that when you act as if you care, you find yourself caring. And when your customer senses that their well-being is important to you, prepare for business to come your way.

PUTTING YOURSELF ON AN EQUAL FOOTING

Because sales is meant to be about partnership and not competition, treat one another as equals. When you meet face to face, eye to eye, and shoulder to shoulder you have an even platform from which to work.

The following suggestions will help you maintain the balance in your partnership:

- **Shaking hands.** When it comes to shaking hands, it's all about the pressure. Too much of a squeeze and you appear domineering or ignorant. Too weak a shake and you come across as lacking in confidence or simply lethargic. You want to mirror the other person's handshake, putting you both on an equal footing.
- **Avoid touching yourself.** Even the slightest covering of your mouth, rubbing of your eyes, or scratching of your nose indicates discomfort. When people are feeling needy, they frequently touch their bodies.
- **Connect with your eyes.** Hold a warm and steady gaze to show you're trustworthy with nothing to hide. Shifty,

steely, and visor-like eyes send negative messages such as dishonesty, insincerity, and hostility.

- **Watch the arms.** How people hold their arms shows how open or closed they are. Avoid crossing them so you don't look defensive. Keep them relaxed by your sides. If you want to demonstrate that you feel comfortable and confident, slightly expand your arms from your sides, filling up your space a little bit more. An inch or two is plenty.

 TELL ME ABOUT YOU

Annette is my mentor, the best boss I ever had, and one of the world's great sales people. Curious, insightful, and consistently gracious in persuading others to join her band, Annette could sell ice to Eskimos, if circumstances required.

I recently introduced Annette to my two most trusted colleagues. Knowing of her celebrated career, both women were excited to meet her. After the drinks arrived, Annette leaned forward, smiled, looked them both in the eye, and opened the conversation by saying "Now, tell me about you." While both women are highly accomplished and respected in their professions, they were in awe. Here they were in front of a legend, and she wanted to know about them. They felt flattered and Annette gained useful insights that she shared with me later. Had we been seeking a sale, we would have nailed it.

PAYING ATTENTION

The way people communicate, including their

- vocal quality
- movements
- gestures
- facial expressions
- breathing patterns

tells you who you're dealing with. When you know that, you can adapt your behaviours to match theirs – to demonstrate empathy and harmony. Once the other person is comfortable with you, you can change gear to take them where you want them to go. Pay attention to the following clues.

Facial Expressions

Smiles in which both the eyes and the mouth are engaged signal acceptance and good feelings. You won't go wrong if you return the pleasure by mirroring back the expression. When someone frowns, wrinkles their nose, and lifts one side of their lip in a sneer, they're showing their displeasure. By quickly reflecting back the expression, you're showing that you relate to their feelings. Hang out too long in that state and you'll start believing that you really are disgruntled, whether you have reason to be or not.

Gestures

Open gestures, in which the arms are held slightly away from the body and the palms of the hands are visible, pointing upward or outward, indicate a receptive mind.

Closed gestures, such as crossed arms, clenched fists, and pointing fingers, suggest a padlocked point of view. If you're receiving negative gestures, change your position by shifting your weight and looking up and away to indicate that you're not that person's punching bag.

Movements

Slow, measured, deliberate movements indicate a careful, considered approach. Quick, jerky movements show tension. Look at the person's face and breathing patterns to discover whether the tension is positive or negative. Positive tension includes excitement, enthusiasm, and exuberance. Negative tension signals anxiety, worry, and fear. Mirror positive movements. Stay calm in the presence of negative tension.

Vocal Patterns

Loud, harsh, bombastic voices punctuated with bits of vulgarity and biased language are unpleasant at best. Unless the person is being totally offensive, smile, laugh at their jokes, and engage in a bit of jolly banter to show that you're an okay person. If the behaviour gets too much, pull away, make your own joke, and suggest that you focus on the business at hand.

Voices that are soft, mumbled, and hard to hear require that you lean in towards the person. If you struggle to grasp what they're saying, watch their lips. If that doesn't clear up the communication, politely ask them to speak up and repeat themselves. After a few times, they may get the hint and smarten up their speech.

Breathing Patterns

Match breathing patterns to demonstrate that you know how the person is feeling. Slow, deep breathing indicates calmness, thoughtfulness, and reflection. Short, shallow breathing is a sign of stress, tension, and excitement. Avoid taking short, shallow breaths for too long as you might feel yourself becoming light-headed, worried, and anxious.

> "There's no lotion or potion that will make sales faster and easier for you – unless your potion is hard work."
>
> *–Jeffrey Gitomer*

Demonstrating that you care about your customer is vital in sales. If you find yourself getting impatient in the process, take on the behaviours of someone who does care – even if you're not in the mood – to show your customers that they matter to you:

- Lower your breathing rate.
- Expand your chest.
- Lean forward.
- Lift your chin slightly.
- Look at the other person as they speak.
- Contain your gestures.
- Calm your face.
- Nod your head.
- Establish an inquisitive mindset.

10

MANAGING OTHERS

"Management's job is to convey leadership's message in a compelling and inspiring way. Not just in meetings, but also by example."

Jeffrey Gitomer

Wouldn't life be easier if everyone did what you told them to do when you wanted them to do it? Sadly, pointing your finger, stamping your feet, and saying "do it because I said so" doesn't work on a sustainable basis.

Every day people find themselves having to manage other people's behaviour and expectations. Whether you're coping with domestic issues, dealing with an uncooperative sales assistant, or are the head honcho of your department, you're always managing others.

As a manager, you have a tough job. What's compelling and inspiring to one person may be a big turnoff for another. Knowing which words and behaviours will spur individuals on to greatness, and which will cause them to crash and burn, requires keen observational skills on your part and a willingness to adapt your behaviour to get the best out of others. If one approach doesn't work, try another. Eventually, you'll discover which behaviours you need to demonstrate in order to elicit the most positive responses from everyone you deal with.

And, while some people may have been taught management skills, not everyone has. Landing in a managerial-type role without any guidance and having to learn the necessary skills while doing the job is not uncommon. Dealing with people problems, overseeing projects, setting clear goals, and coaching individuals along the way are just some of the challenges people face every time they get out of bed. For some, these skills come easily. For others, they are less natural. For any manager, practised or not, adopting behaviours that exhibit power and authority – and being able to express encouragement and voice disapproval while demonstrating respect and patience – are all part of a day's work.

> ❝ **Manage your team well and success is yours for the taking. Manage them poorly and prepare for the worst.** ❞

If you want to become a 5-star manager, the following steps will get you started. While the behaviours listed are simple in theory, you may find some of the recommendations difficult. For example, if you're more comfortable hanging out in the background with your head down and your role requires that you stand up front and be heard, you might struggle. Press on. With purpose, patience, and practice, you'll get there.

Demonstrating Respect

Number one rule: treat others with respect. When people feel that you respect and value them and the contribution they make, they'll walk the extra mile, tote the extra bale, and do whatever it takes to get the job done. Even if you don't like the people you're dealing with, when you treat them as if you value them as individuals and the contribution they bring to their work and your life, they respond in a positive way.

To show people that you respect them, adopt the following behaviours.

Facial Expressions

- Steady, comfortable eye contact.
- Facial muscles engaged and relaxed.

- Smiling at appropriate times.
- Features remain calm.

Gestures

- Considerate of personal space (neither too close nor too far away).
- Head tilts when listening.
- Face the other person.
- Shoulders and feet point towards the other person.
- Focus on the other person completely when listening.
- Allow other person to speak without interrupting.
- Use open gestures, showing the palms of your hands.
- Fingers relaxed and separated.
- Nod in understanding, agreement, and encouragement.
- Match and mirror (see Chapter 4) the other person's non-verbal behaviours.

Vocal Patterns

- Appropriate volume, neither so soft that they struggle to hear you nor so loud that they need ear protectors.
- Courteous tones.
- Polite language.
- Clear enunciation.
- Correct pronunciation.

"I am not interested in power for power's sake, but I'm interested in power that is moral, that is right and that is good."

–Martin Luther King, Jr.

Displaying Power

People in positions of power have a tough row to hoe. One step too far right and you come across as Attila the Hun. Too far left and you resemble Eeyore. You have to claim your space while encouraging others to support you in doing so. Your aim is to display a balance of commanding and humble non-verbal behaviours.

Facial Expressions

- Cheek muscles engaged.
- Comfortable, connected eye contact.
- Firm lips.
- Loose jaw.
- Mouth lifted at the sides.
- Head held steadily.

Gestures

- Fluid, steady, unrushed.
- Hands kept between chest and waist level.
- Palms facing down (be careful with this one, while it demonstrates confidence and shows that you know what you're talking about, the gesture conveys rigidity if fingers are tight).
- Steepled fingers (palms facing each other with just the fingertips touching).
- Hands held behind the back.
- Raised chest.
- Chin lifted.

- Elbows somewhat extended to fill the surrounding space.
- Straight, upright posture.
- Slow, deep breathing.

Steepling the fingers can be an indication of displaying power.

Vocal Patterns

- Deep tones.
- Rich, resonant sounds.
- Appropriate volume.
- Even speech pattern.
- Fluid stream of sound.
- Measured pace.
- Clear articulation.
- Uses pauses and silence.
- Respectful choice of words.

Acting With Authority

To be dubbed an authority carries implications of experience and expertise. Because of those two kudos, there's always the temptation to take yourself too seriously and slip into arrogance. As with power, when you behave with strength and dignity without displaying too much self-satisfaction, people tend to respond to you in a favourable way.

Facial Expressions

- Smooth forehead.
- Steady gaze.
- Eyebrows held horizontally to show strength and purpose.
- Eyebrows raised in curiosity and attentiveness.
- Unclenched jaw.
- Firm lips.
- Chin slightly lifted.
- Cool, dry skin.

Gestures

- Hand gestures controlled.
- Pointing with whole hand rather than index finger.
- Fingers relaxed.
- Palms open and facing outward.
- Chopping gestures, in which the fingers are held together:
  - to emphasize a point, separating an idea into two categories
  - to clarify a fact
  - to indicate disagreement
  - to show certainty and rigidity.

- Beware of slipping into a sense of dominance or defiance when using pointing and chopping gestures. While you may point a finger in the air to add emphasis to your words, don't point or jab your finger at someone. Doing so is confrontational, invasive, and offensive, and makes you look aggressive, angry, and arrogant. That said, a wink combined with a playful finger point is a pleasant expression of approval or acknowledgement.

Vocal Patterns

- Sound is well supported.
- Strong emphasis on words and phrases.
- Tone is rich and resonant.
- Sentences end on a solid, low note.
- Voice is free of obstructions.
- Words are clearly articulated.
- Speech is concise.
- Pace is slow and rhythmic.
- Language is respectful.
- No verbal tags or qualifiers, such as:
    - Let's go with that plan, *okay?*
    - *I guess* this will meet with their approval, *don't you?*
    - I think this is a solid plan, *if you know what I mean?*
    - *I just thought* this would work, *won't it?*

Offering Encouragement

Whether you're managing your child, training a dog, or supervising a team of individuals, most personalities respond better to words of encouragement than they do to disparaging comments and dismissive actions. The following non-verbal behaviours help jolly people along.

Facial Expressions

- Muscles engaged.
- Eyebrows lifted.
- Eyes widened.
- Smiling.
- Eye contact comfortable and steady.

Movements and Gestures

- Body leans in.
- Supportive hand signals such as thumbs up, the okay sign (in which the index finger and thumb make a circle), back-patting, palm-slapping, knuckle-bumping, and hand-pumping.
- Head nodding quickly to show interest and excitement.
- Slow nods to show that you're absorbing and supporting what you observe.
- Movements may be excited, quick, and spontaneous or calm and measured, depending on how the other person responds.

Vocal Patterns

- High pitch coming from upper registers.
- Supported breath control.
- Excited tone.

- Quick delivery.
- Short bursts of words and phrases.
- Louder volume than usual.
- Words of praise.
- Inspiring language.
- Supportive language to elicit further information, such as "That's interesting, tell me more about that…" or "So, then what happened…" "What do you think would be the best approach to take?"
- Urge the other person to continue speaking with words like "I see, um hm, yes, ah" to show that you're listening.

Showing Disapproval

"Disapproval is a very important factor in all progress. There has really never been any progress without it."

–James Henry Breasted

Like a quick crack of the whip, showing disapproval is sometimes necessary to get people to pay attention, clean up their act, and get on with the job. Whether you're at the receiving end or are giving out the red cards to someone else, these signs are sure signs of displeasure, dissatisfaction, and discontent.

Facial Expressions

- Scowling.
- Tightness around the eyes.
- Rolling eyes (this rude gesture also shows contempt and disrespect).

- Flared nostrils.
- Steely gaze.
- Tenseness around the mouth.
- Clenched jaw.

Gestures

- Head tilts forward and downward.
- Body pulls back.
- Fists clench.
- Pointing or jabbing with index finger.
- Arms fold across the body.
- Finger tapping.
- Feet remain fixed in place.
- Toes tap.
- Breathing is short and shallow.

Vocal Patterns

- Tight tones.
- Clipped speech.
- Strict language.
- Short sentences.
- Breathing can be either slow and deep or shallow and quick, depending on the intensity of the emotion.

"Patience, persistence and perspiration make an unbeatable combination for success."

–Napoleon Hill

THE PATIENT PROFESSIONAL

One of Libby's greatest talents lies in her patience. Whether directing plays starring world-class actors, collaborating on a writing project with someone from a different culture, or teaching Shakespeare to university students, Libby approaches her work with calmness, curiosity, and respect for the people she works with and the task at hand. Her voice seldom raises, even when she has to repeat her message several times; her language is always respectful, even if she wants to tell someone to stop acting like an idiot; and her facial expressions are warm, open, and non-judgemental. She emits few scowls or clenched fists, and I've never seen her stomp her foot in censure. Instead, her words are supportive, her body language is open, and her positive attitude gets everyone performing at their very best.

Expressing Patience

Facial Expressions

- Wide eyes, brows lifted with interest.
- Comfortable eye contact.
- Soft focus.
- Calm forehead.
- Cheek muscles engaged.
- Mouth soft and lifted at the sides.
- Expressions mostly still.

Gestures

- Head tilts when listening.
- Head upright when giving instructions or information.
- Mouth remains closed to avoid interrupting.
- Body leans forward.
- Open palm gestures.
- Fingers and feet relaxed and still.
- Arms and legs uncrossed.
- Breathing pattern is slow, deep, and regular.

Vocal Patterns

- Warm tones.
- Soft spoken.
- Clear articulation.
- Simple sentences.
- Using the pause to give people time to reflect.
- Non-threatening language.
- Slow, deep breathing.

> "Power tends to corrupt and absolute power corrupts absolutely."
> *–Lord Acton*

Sidestepping the Pitfalls

All too often, managers become intoxicated by their position and abuse the power that comes with it. With a plethora of people acting like groupies in order to garner the manager's approval, the temptation to take advantage of them can be appealing. Don't. Positional power is a privilege. When it comes your way, act judiciously, avoiding the following behaviours.

1. **Playing favourites.** Showing your preference for one individual over another is unfair, divisive, and damaging to your reputation and the team's morale.

   Behaviours to avoid

   - Spending too much time with favoured individuals.
   - Sharing inside jokes with some and not others.
   - Looking at certain individuals and not others when you're speaking.
   - Disclosing information to certain people and not to others.
   - Nodding, winking, and smiling only with selected individuals.
   - Touching certain individuals in a friendly way (for example, back-slapping, high-fiving, knuckle-bumping) and not others.

2. **Losing your cool.** Focus on being rational and logical, not emotional.

   Behaviours to avoid

   - Shouting.
   - Name calling.
   - Finger pointing.
   - Fist slamming.
   - Finger drumming.
   - Jiggling feet.
   - Short, shallow breathing.

3. **Micromanaging.** As someone who manages the performance of others, your goal is to lead people in solving problems, not micromanaging them to finish a task.

   Behaviours to avoid

   - Physically leaning over others while they're working.
   - Pointing or wagging your index finger in someone's direction.
   - Tensing your facial expressions, including
     - pursing your lips
     - squinting your eyes
     - frowning
     - flaring your nostrils
     - tightening your jaw
     - breathing in a short, jagged pattern.

4. **Dealing with conflict.** Much of management requires addressing or adjudicating conflict situations. The ability to resolve conflict without shedding blood is a core management – and life – skill.

   Behaviours to avoid

   - Raising your voice.
   - Pointing your finger at someone.
   - Making a fist.
   - Scowling.
   - Speaking derisively.
   - Tensing your body.
   - Crossing your arms.
   - Clenching your jaw.
   - Short, shallow breathing.

A final thought before concluding this chapter: **provide feedback.** Whenever you're managing others, whether they're the people who clean your home, your team at the office, or your crew on the shop floor, providing feedback is a core skill you need to put in your tool kit. Make sure you focus on the situation and not the person, and keep your words positive and supportive. Language such as "I noticed that..." and "I felt... when you..." keep the feedback focused on the behaviour rather than on the individual.

Behaviours to adopt

Facial expressions:

- smooth forehead
- open eyes, comfortably focused on the other person
- loose jaw
- relaxed lips
- gentle smile when appropriate
- calm expression.

Movements and gestures:

- facing the person, with feet and shoulders pointing towards them
- holding head upright
- nodding in acknowledgement and understanding
- maintaining eye contact
- small gestures to highlight points
- open palms
- deep, slow breathing.

When giving feedback, avoid using the word "but", as in: "You spoke clearly when you talked about the water crisis, but you could have made your points more concisely."

The recipient will only remember the negative message – what came after the "but" – and not your positive comments. Replace "but" with a full stop or the word "and".

For example: "You spoke clearly when you talked about the water crisis. The next time, aim to make your points more concisely." Or: "You spoke clearly when you talked about the water crisis and the next time aim to make your points more concisely."

While this may feel awkward at first, after practising positive phrasing you'll notice a positive reaction in the recipient's response.

11

ATTRACTING OTHERS

"I speak two languages, Body and English."

Mae West

I n every situation in which you engage with other people, your non-verbal behaviour gets in on the act. Whether you're trying to get a waiter's attention, end an argument, or stand up to a bully, the pace of your movements, the type of posture you adopt, the gestures that you use, and the quality of your voice influence the way you deliver your message and how others perceive you.

At work, keeping your body language as neutral as possible is advisable to prevent others from questioning your motives. Touching in the workplace, for example, is discouraged. That's unfortunate, because a touch can convey encouragement and praise. It can also convey sexual interest. To prevent your reputation from being tarnished, keep your hands to yourself during working hours. How you move and gesture in your free time is your business.

Because I trust that you have a life outside of the office and because friends, clients and colleagues frequently ask me how they can attract others with their non-verbal behaviour, I decided to include a chapter on how to appeal to others and how to tell when they're coming onto you. What we're really talking about here is flirting. How to flirt your way into someone's good books. Because men and women send out and respond to signals differently, I have broken this chapter into two sections: one aimed at attracting a woman and the other geared for appealing to a man.

A few pointers to remember about sending positive signals through your body language before delving into the specifics of flirting:

- face the other person and lean towards them
- establish eye contact and focus only on them

- smile
- nod to show interest
- use open gestures
- keep your body calm.

"If you don't flirt, you're probably dead inside."

–Katharine Towne

Attracting a Woman

Women respond particularly positively to three qualities:

- charisma
- good manners
- a great sense of humour.

Here is a list of behaviours that will ensure you at least get a second look if not a full-blown romance.

For every word you say, allow her to say five. While exceptions to this rule may be found, for the most part, women tend to talk more than men. They thrive on extra air time and will appreciate your giving it to them.

Ask her questions about herself and demonstrate interest. Look at her when she speaks. Smile. Nod your head. Lean towards her. Behaving this way will make her feel special, and prone to like you.

Tell her you find something artistic about her. While you may find this an odd suggestion, tilting your head and smiling while telling her that her smile reminds you of the Mona Lisa, or that her hair resembles Botticelli's Venus is bound to stir her interest in you. In addition to being both intelligent and innovative, demonstrating your knowledge of the arts implies that you are knowledgeable and can engage with topics other than sports, the weather, or celebrity gossip. *A word of* *warning:* avoid getting too technical. Saying that she resembles a painting from Picasso's Cubist period might put her in a huff.

Let your eyes smile. A lingering look with a soft smile communicates your interest without you having to say a word. You might want to practise this look as too much intensity can be scary while not enough won't get you anywhere.

Offer her genuine and original compliments. Point out something nice about her hands, her hair, the way she's put her outfit together. You could compliment her on her choice of perfume and try guessing which one she's wearing. On that note, be sure that you know your perfumes, or you could come across as a bit of a creep.

Pay attention to details. Note what she's wearing, from her jewellery to her shoes. When you see her again and are able to refer to the earrings she was wearing when you first met, she'll feel special that you noticed, remembered, and commented.

Give her space. Don't lean so far into her personal space that she feels crowded. Resist touching her until she leans in towards you. Then you could casually touch her lower arm or shoulder in a brief pat. You can give her a hug too. Keep it non-threatening by not pressing your body into hers.

Communicate with eloquence. Speak in clear, coherent sentences using vocal variety to add interest and emphasis to your message. If you suffer from sloppy speech, such as poor articulation, practise. Breathe slowly and deeply to create a calm and receptive environment.

Have a laugh. Laughter is a way of making people feel comfortable and creating a casual, friendly atmosphere. Having a laugh on yourself makes you appear honest and humble.

Chill out. Move slowly and with purpose. Short, jerky gestures are awkward and make you appear insecure. Tight fists and fidgeting fingers indicate tension. Calm, smooth, open gestures in which you show the palms of your hands are appealing and encourage honest communication.

Mirror her behaviour. Create a harmonious state by responding to what you observe. If she pulls back and turns away from you, she's sending signals that she's not interested so don't force the subject. If she turns towards you, smiles, and leans forward in your direction, reflect back those behaviours. If she pulls back, you pull back too. Let her take the lead. Once she shows you how far you can go, go there. As long as you behave in a respectful way, she'll keep the door open.

Make her feel special. Lean towards her, smile, look her in the eye, lower your voice, and tell her that you think she's a one-off, an exceptional person, and is sizzling hot. Few women will walk away from that compliment. Focus your eyes only on her and don't even think about looking at anyone else in the room.

"Not only is her body language revealing, but so are her silences... It's how she doesn't say things verbally that I find exceedingly communicative."

–Laurence Kardish

Appealing to a Man

The number one criterion for engaging a man's attention is to demonstrate **sincerity**. Research shows that the best-liked and most successful flirting strategy is having an open, honest conversation with the goal of getting to know someone. Men react favourably when you:

- let your guard down
- share who you are
- make an emotional connection.

How can you do that? Through your behaviour. Because men aren't good at picking up on subtle signals, show your interest by slightly exaggerating gestures and facial expressions to guide them.

Behaviours that men respond favourably to include:

- comfortable, engaged eye contact
- genuine smiles
- self-touching gestures, such as licking your lips, flicking your hair, and stroking your throat.

In contrast, avoiding eye contact or staring with a disengaged expression, clenching your fists, crossing your arms, and turning your face and body away are signs of disinterest.

Below are a few tips for letting your guard down and making an emotional connection.

Demonstrate poise and confidence in your actions. Men find strong and sensuous movements – like those of strippers and pole dancers – more appealing than those that are timid and tentative. Don't get me wrong: I'm not suggesting you remove your clothes or extend your leg over your head, at least not at the first meeting. I am suggesting that you move with purpose and pride.

Shoulders back, chin up. Even if you're quaking inside, slightly arch your back and lift your chin to make you feel and appear confident and comfortable within yourself. When you open yourself up physically you let down your guard, creating a state where emotional connections can happen.

Establish eye contact. Scan the space before honing in on the cute guy in the corner. When you connect, hold the eye contact for a moment, then look down. Look at him again, letting your eyes lock onto his. Look down once more, and when you look at him again, hold the eye contact. (Men are simple creatures and need three attempts at something before trusting that it's real.) This should take no more than two minutes. If he doesn't look at you to begin with, or has shown no interest by the third glance, move on. There are plenty of other fish to be caught.

Smile. Once you've got his attention, offer a mischievous smile. Flirting is about being playful, light-hearted, and spirited.

Touch. Making a physical connection builds comfort. As long as you touch appropriately. Keep your hands off his thighs until you've gotten to know one another. Touch his arm when making a point. If he has fluff on his jacket or his tie is askew, fix it. This type of physical contact shows warmth and care.

Voice. Put variety into your voice. Pause. Relax. Slow down. Speed up. Breathe. A fun and playful voice is engaging, interesting, and likeable.

Give the guy a break. Engaging with you when you're with your friends is tough for men. If you've caught eyes and you're both showing interest with cheeky smiles and still he's resisting crossing the room to speak with you, he might give you the "wave over" inviting you to join him in his space. Respond by returning the gesture. You may go back and forth a few times before he succumbs and approaches you. At that point you simply say, with a charming smile, "I just wanted to say hi." If he's a good guy, he'll be enchanted and will stay with you. If he doesn't come over, he's not worth your effort.

 FLIRTING HER WAY THROUGH LIFE

Lisa is a vivacious woman. While she's realistic about life's ups and downs, she exudes positive energy. Whether having a quick chat with the hostess at her favourite restaurant or engaging with C-suite executives, Lisa projects warmth, interest, and a get-up-and-go attitude. People are drawn to her because of her upbeat attitude, ready smile, and the twinkle in her eye. Her young daughter once said to her: "Mummy, you just flirt with life!"

FINAL SUGGESTIONS FOR ATTRACTING OTHERS THROUGH YOUR BODY LANGUAGE

In a nutshell, attracting others – or flirting, for short – is about making other people feel good about themselves. It's about demonstrating warmth and trustworthiness. It's about being fun, light, and playful. Cool. Now, how do you do that? Whether you want to attract a man or a woman, the following behaviours demonstrate your interest:

1. **Make comfortable eye contact.** When you look at someone, really look at them. Wandering eyes are a big turn off, leaving the other person feeling less than good about themselves. Be careful not to over-look and stare, which is just odd.

2. **Widen your eyes.** Raising your brows and opening your eyes demonstrates interest.

3. **Smile.** When a person smiles they appear approachable, trustworthy, and playful. A genuine smile, in which the eyes are engaged as well as the mouth, lights up your face. Smiling draws people in and when the smile is pointed in their direction, makes them feel special.

4. **Lean in.** Moving your body towards the other person shows that you're interested enough in them to enter their territory. That being said, don't go so far that they can taste your coffee breath. Take it slowly.

5. **Make your movements smooth and languid.** Short, jerky gestures are a turn off.

Mirroring a subtle touch shows friendliness.

6. **Maintain an upright posture.** An erect position demonstrates energy, interest, and confidence. A slumped posture indicates apathy, listlessness, and boredom.

7. **Focus on them.** No fidgeting, no shuffling, no looking away.

8. **Touch gently and discreetly.** A subtle touch like a shoulder push or tap is friendly and non-threatening, whereas touching someone around the waist or forearm is more direct. Touching someone on the face is quite intimate and groping is not recommended. Keep your touches gentle and informal. A face-to-face hug demonstrates warmth and openness.

While men may be slower in picking up signs and signals than women, both genders want to feel special, attractive, and appreciated. The suggestions offered in this chapter provide you with a clear path for reaching that goal.

To hone your flirting skills you have to practise. If you're too shy to flirt with the person you have a crush on, practise on strangers, preferably people you won't see again or that you see only infrequently. Try out your techniques with the cute guy at the checkout counter, the pretty woman on the bus, or anyone who is unthreatening and willing to let you engage with them. Flirting with a friend is weird and could make them wonder about your intentions.

12

DETECTING LIES

"I'm hopeless at telling lies. I can attempt strategic ones in order not to hurt people's feelings, but then I'll blow it 10 minutes later."

Nicholas Haslam

ere's the story: your boss/client tells you that despite the economy/merger/sales figures, your job is safe. While you'd like to believe what you hear, something in the delivery sets off alarms in your head.

Previously held beliefs that you could tell someone was lying simply by

- lack of eye contact
- fidgeting
- sweating

no longer hold true. Firstly, before making a judgement, you have to observe a *cluster of behaviours*. Secondly, rather than looking for signs of nervousness, research tells us to look for *signs of thinking*. Why is that?

Lying takes time and effort. Someone who is lying has to (1) make up a story and (2) deliver it in a way that convinces the listener. That creative people make the best liars should come as no surprise when you consider that the basic requirements of lying are

- imagination
- concentration
- a good memory.

Some people struggle to recognize when they're being lied to because they (1) listen for what they want to hear, (2) believe that others wouldn't lie, and/or (3) are uncomfortable judging someone else. If that's you, tune up your antennae. People aren't always to be trusted.

"Reality is easy. It's deception that's the hard work."

–Lauryn Hill

Figuring out if someone is lying to you is easier if you know the person. Because you're already familiar with how they behave in stressful situations, you have a baseline to work from. Whether you know the person or not, if you think they might be telling you a big, fat porky, pay attention to

- facial expressions
- gestures
- speech patterns
- word choice.

Facial Expressions

- **Eye contact.** Contrary to popular belief, a liar does not always avoid eye contact. Frequently, they will deliberately make eye contact to appear honest and sincere. In addition, their rate of blinking reduces as they concentrate on telling their tale.

- **Mouth movements.** If the person you think is being dishonest is licking or pulling on their *lips*, you could be right. The same holds true if someone is scratching their *nose*, or tugging at their *ears*. A person telling a falsehood is under stress. Blood rushes to certain areas and triggers a sensation of cold or itching as part of the flight-or-fight response.

- **Micro expressions.** These tiny movements, barely discernible to the naked eye, flash across the face, exposing a person's real feelings, regardless of what they're saying. To learn more about micro expressions, turn to the work of Paul Ekman at www.paulekman.com.

Gestures

In addition to verbal clues, non-verbal signals that can indicate someone is being economical with the truth include the behaviours listed below. Before reading any further, note that these cues should only be considered as signs of deceit when demonstrated in direct response to your questions.

- **Fidgeting.** People who are afraid of being found out tend to fidget, either with their own body or with random objects around them.

- **Disconnects.** If someone nods his head in the affirmative while saying "no", or shakes his head in a negative response while he's saying "yes", you're witnessing a disconnect, or an incongruence, which is frequently a sign of deception.

- **Delayed affirmation.** People who are avoiding telling the truth may hesitate before nodding in response to a question. People who are telling the truth tend to nod in support of a statement or answer the question at the same time as they're nodding.

- **Hiding.** Covering up a lie is a natural inclination. If you notice the other person covering his mouth or eyes while responding, chances are he's covering up the truth. The same clue can be noticed when the person simply shuts his eyes while answering your questions, indicating that he doesn't want to see your reaction to his fabrication.

- **Shifting anchor points.** Anchor points are parts that hold a person in a particular spot or position. If someone is standing, his feet are anchor points. If someone is seated, his bottom becomes his anchor point. When the anchor points start to shift, the desire to deceive can be the cause.

- **A lack of mirroring.** People naturally mirror the behaviour of others with whom they're interacting as a means of creating rapport and demonstrating interest (see Chapter 4 for more about mirroring). Mirroring may lessen as the person fabricating the story concentrates on creating another reality for the listener. For example, someone telling you a tale may lean away from you as an unconscious sign of wanting to get out of the situation or not wanting to give more information than absolutely necessary. When people have nothing to hide they tend to lean towards the listener.

- **Looking away** as a defensive ploy.

- **Few arm and leg movements.**

- **Sweating, trembling, blushing, and difficulty in swallowing** can be further signs of discomfort as a result of telling untruths.

Leaning back and looking away can suggest a desire to get out of the situation.

Vocal Patterns

Speech Patterns

- **Failing to answer the question.** Dodging a direct question indicates that the person is trying to come up with a good response because he doesn't want to come clean.

- **Denial.** Ask the question, "Did you do it?" If the response is anything other than a simple "yes" or "no", the subject is most likely lying. Saying "I didn't do anything/It wasn't me/I didn't do it" is a psychological way of avoiding telling a flat out fib.

- **Pace of speech** indicates if someone is lying, by being either faster or slower than normal. Tension may result in a higher **pitch** than usual. You may detect a **quaver** in the tone.

- **Stuttering and stammering** are also indicators that something's not quite right, as is injecting **stalling tactics**, such as

  - deflection
  - going on the offensive
  - omitting relevant facts
  - repeating or asking for the question to be repeated.

- **Timing and duration of response.** While honest answers tend to come quickly from memory, someone telling a tale needs time to mentally review what they've told others in order to remain consistent and to add new details when necessary. That being said, someone inventing a story may rattle off a response because she (1) has rehearsed her answer or (2) is just thinking up a quick reply to get it over with.

Word Choice

Someone aiming to deceive *restates* what has already been established and doesn't reveal much else. In addition, listen for clues such as:

- **Repeating** your exact words when responding to your questions. For example, someone who is lying would likely respond to your question "Did you authorize that transaction?" with "Yes/No, I did/did not authorize that transaction."

- **Filler words,** such as

Or, if the answer is more complex than a simple "yes" or "no", a **confrontational style** including

- "It depends on what you mean by…"
- "Who told you that?"/"Where did you get that information?"

- "What are you talking about?"
- "Why are you wasting my time with this?"

WHY POLITICIANS LIE

Is there such a thing as an honest politician? From experience and research, I would say "No". So, why do they lie? Because we want them to. "Say, WHAT!" you may exclaim in outrage. Hear me out. While someone is running for political office, they will tell you what you want to hear. They will lie FOR you, which you perceive as different from lying TO you. The candidate is the representative of your party or ideology, and believing him/her allows you to remain a member in good standing of your tribe. To social animals, like humans, tribe matters. We depend on the tribe for our health and safety. Therefore, we agree with our tribal leaders even when they tell a whopper, and we wiggle our way into seeing the facts as they do, rather than taking an objective viewpoint. Most people don't seek objectivity; they want safety, social cohesion, and survival.

- **Avoiding using contractions.** For example, saying "I did *not*..." rather than "I didn't..." is an attempt to make the message absolutely clear.
- **Changing the subject**, using **humour** or **sarcasm** to avoid giving a direct answer to the question.
- **Questioning you** to get the heat off them.

- **Not making sense.** When people lie they get nervous and make up stories that don't always make sense. Their sentences are muddled, they tend to stop mid-phrase, change the subject, start again, and fail to finish their sentences.

- **Too much information.** People who lie tend to provide too much detail in their desperation to get you to believe what they're saying.

- **Impersonal language.** In an attempt to distance themselves from their deceitfulness, people who are lying rely on impersonal language, reducing the number of times they use the words "I/me/mine" and replacing people's proper names with "him/her".

- **Being overly polite.** Showering you with compliments, or responding to just one of your questions with a "Yes, sir/mam" is an indicator that the person is trying to win your favour so you'll believe them.

- **Introducing high powers.** People who start talking about God as in "I swear to God" or "As God is my witness" are, as psychologists say, "dressing up the lie".

"You can fool all the people some of the time, and some of the people all the time, but you cannot fool all the people all the time."
–Abraham Lincoln

A warning to sleuths in training: although the indicators listed above are signs of deception, be careful in your analysis. A number of reasons could be causing someone to appear to be lying when the signs could simply be due to

- embarrassment
- shyness

- awkwardness
- anxiety
- a sense of shame/inferiority.

Someone suffering from stress can easily be mistaken for a liar, as both states share some of the same indicators. Therefore, make sure that you base your judgements on a "cluster" of deceptive behaviours and reactions, as there is no single sign saying "That's a lie!"

Try the following if you think someone is lying to you:

- Have the person tell their story backwards, starting at the end and thoroughly working their way back to the beginning. Tell them to be as complete and detailed as possible. Even people who are well schooled in deception find this challenge difficult, as the exercise requires a lot of mental effort to stick to the story while scrutinizing your response.
- Ask open-ended questions to get them to provide as much detail and information as you can get out of them. Questions such as "Can you tell me more about...?" and "So, tell me exactly..." Begin by asking general questions before diving into the specifics.
- Don't interrupt. Use silence to encourage the other person to speak. Someone telling a tale needs confirmation that you're buying what he's selling. Because silence offers no feedback on whether or not you believe what's being said, the liar, in his discomfort, will likely keep talking to fill the void and the chances of him slipping up increase.
- To make sure you're getting all the information you need, ask a catch-all question such as "Is there anything else I need to know about this?"

13

DEALING WITH CONFLICT, AGGRESSION, AND CONFRONTATION

"For good ideas and true innovation, you need human interaction, conflict, argument, debate."

Margaret Heffernan

Conflict. Aggression. Confrontation. For many, these are words of dread, while for others, they are the breakfast of champions.

Before going any further, let's do a little spot check.

- Do you accept that conflict, change, and arguments are a natural part of life?
- Do you seek to find peaceful solutions to disagreements?

If you answered yes to the above questions, congratulations. I trust your behaviour reflects respect for others and the desire to build rapport in your quest to produce mutually satisfying results. (For more about rapport building, go to Chapter 3.)

On the contrary:

- Are you a people pleaser?
- Are you prone to anxiety?
- Do you fear conflict and negative feelings, including anger?
- When you feel upset, do you sweep your problems under the rug?
- Do you resist expressing your emotions?
- Do you struggle to ask for what you want?
- Do you frequently feel resentful?

If you answered yes to any of these questions, read on to discover *how to think and act* as you move from avoiding to accepting conflict, seeing it as the beginning of a profitable and productive relationship.

66 Conflict and confrontation can be exciting and enlightening. 99

Disputes provide opportunities to hear the other side of the story and view the situation from a different standpoint. In addition, conflict and confrontation provide you with an opportunity to present your views, your needs, and your concerns in a clear and respectful way that the other person can understand.

HOW DO I BEGIN?

Begin by considering *your relationship with conflict*. Is conflict something you welcome or would you rather eat crushed glass before entering into a dispute? Perhaps being right is part of your DNA and you relish the chance to crush the opposition.

66 The values and beliefs you carry into a conflict impact on your actions and responses to other people's behaviour. 99

Confrontation is a natural part of life. Conflict can be seen as the catalyst for keeping people curious. Without conflicting opinions, life would be a rather predictable place. Differences in opinion are good, in that they expand a person's thinking and lead to better-informed choices.

If you *keep in mind your goals* and *listen to what's important to the other person*, you can achieve win–win results without shedding blood. (You can gain tips for active listening in Chapter 2.)

All too often, people view conflict as a negative battle of wills, with a winner and a loser at the finish line. If that's you, **change your attitude.** Make a conscious decision to perceive conflict as an opportunity to treat other people with respect as you learn about their differing values, needs, and concerns. In addition, you can treat conflict as an opportunity to express your needs, values, and concerns too. ALWAYS in a respectful way. Avoid getting all hot under the collar and snarling like a rabid dog. This won't win you any friends and while you may win a battle that way, you'll lose the war. Instead, when your viewpoint is different from the other person's, remain cool, calm, and in control of your actions, expressions, and your choice of vocabulary. Keep in mind your desired outcomes, the main one being to achieve results that please both parties.

> **❝Your attitude towards conflict and how you act that out determines whether or not you are successful in achieving mutually satisfying results.❞**

When conflict is at hand:

- Aim to understand the other person's perspective.
- Be willing to accept that you and others may have a different point of view.

- Make it your purpose to achieve an outcome that satisfies both of you.

- Be prepared to devote time and patience to the process.

- Unless your core values are under attack, be willing to compromise for the purpose of producing results that satisfy all parties.

 GOING NOWHERE FAST

As I was driving through rush-hour traffic, I was listening to a radio programme in which Roger, the host, called his neighbour Kevin to ask that he turn off some of his outdoor Christmas lights. Roger and his young family had recently moved into the neighbourhood and were celebrating their first Christmas in their new home.

When Roger explained that Kevin's coloured flashing lights in his back garden kept his children awake, Kevin suggested that Roger put eye shades on the children. Kevin continued by saying, with increasing volume and pace, that his decorations were a local attraction and that his display had been growing in popularity over the years. People came from miles around to see his lights, another point which bothered Roger, as the extra traffic caused parking problems and increased noise on the block. As the pitch of Kevin's voice rose and his language became redder and more aggressive, Roger matched his adversary's tone and behaviour, including threatening to remove Kevin's prized decoration, a larger-than-life size blow up Father Christmas that Kevin places in his front garden every year.

As the confrontation became more like a Jerry Springer nightmare, with neither party listening to the other, I had to change stations. Was Roger winding Kevin up for entertainment purposes? Would Kevin make good on his threats? Whichever, I found the stress of dodging motorcycles and 18-wheelers while listening to an aggressive confrontation distracting and disturbing in equal measures.

In situations like Roger and Kevin's, emotions are running high, reputations are at stake, vested interests are under attack, and you're feeling threatened. Your natural instinct is either to

- freeze
- fight
- run away.

None of which solve the problem.

Business people, people who work in teams, organizational representatives, and anyone else who engages with other individuals know that from time to time differences in needs, concerns, and opinions occur. People who have successful relationships tend to have a healthy view of themselves and are respectful of others. Rather than shying away from conflict, they encourage it, understanding that different points of view add value when decisions are being made.

When feeling threatened, your natural instinct to fight back is unlikely to solve the problem.

When you find yourself in a conflict situation, unless guns are being fired in your direction, stay put even when the following behaviours are coming your way.

Facial Expressions

- Tightness around mouth and eyes.
- Frowning, scowling, and glaring.
- Lowered eyebrows.
- Tense jaw.
- Flushed skin colour.
- Hot and perspiring.

Gestures

- Pointing and jabbing fingers.
- Crossed arms and legs.
- Clenched fists.
- Short, shallow breathing.

- Quick.
- Jerky.
- Encroaching on your space.

Vocal Patterns

- Loud.
- Harsh.
- Tight.
- Threatening or abusive language.
- Quick pace.
- High pitch.

Hold your ground and face your adversary. Remain silent and do not interrupt. Once the other person has spent their energy, adopt the following behaviours to help lead to a positive outcome.

Facial Expressions

- Smooth forehead.
- Relaxed muscles around eyes and mouth.
- Gently closed mouth.
- Loosely held jaw.

Gestures

- Head nodding with understanding and acceptance.
- Open hand gestures.
- Arms uncrossed.
- Chest exposed.
- Slow, deep breathing.

Vocal Patterns

- Low tones.
- Measured.
- Firm.
- Steady.
- Reassuring language.

I know this may feel uncomfortable. Do it anyhow. At this point you don't want to mirror and match the other person's behaviours for fear of escalating the conflict further. Give them time to put their case forward without arguing or interrupting. Actively listen and aim to understand how the other person is experiencing the world. By treating them fairly and presenting your position in a way that the other person can understand, you are on your way to reaching mutually desirable outcomes through constructive conflict. (See Chapter 2 for more about active listening.)

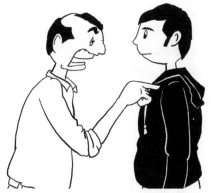

In a conflict situation, actively listen and give the other person time to put their case forward.

"Man must evolve for all human conflict a method which rejects revenge, aggression and retaliation. The foundation of such a method is love."

–Martin Luther King, Jr.

Before entering into a dispute, find out as much about the other party – and yourself – as you can by asking:

- What are my values?
- What do I want to achieve as a result of this interaction?
- What's important to me about that?
- What are the other person's values?
- What do they want to achieve?
- What's important to them about that?
- What am I willing to do to reach my desired outcomes?
- What else can I do?
- What am I not willing to do?
- What am I willing to give up?

This exercise takes time, patience, and a willingness to dig deep. The benefit of doing so is that you will meet conflict with grace and generosity, court confrontation when doing so is beneficial, and produce the kind of positive results that people talk about with respect and admiration.

14

CROSS-CULTURAL COMMUNICATION

"We are, at almost every point of our day, immersed in cultural diversity: faces, clothes, smells, attitudes, values, traditions, behaviours, beliefs, rituals."

Randa Abdel-Fattah

What do Asia, Africa, America, Allianz, Amex, and Avon have in common? They all begin with the letter A. Beyond that, differences abound and are reflected in the way people behave. Even within the same country and company, values vary and people struggle to understand one another's attitudes, beliefs, and behaviours. How can you be expected to engage comfortably with people whose cultures are so unlike your own?

The simple answer is: *treat all people with respect and aim to establish rapport.* (See Chapter 3 for ways of creating rapport.) Be curious and seek to learn what you don't know. Rather than judging and finding fault, approach the challenge of communicating across cultures as an opportunity to discover how other people view the world. Appreciate that one culture is neither more right nor more wrong than another; they're simply different.

❝Attitudes, beliefs, values, background, customs, ethnicity, principles, and traditions all impact on how people behave. ❞

The world is populated with over 7 billion people, each one perceiving the world based on the culture in which they were raised. These cultures will be, for the most part, different from yours. Because culture impacts on communication, you're going to bump into a lot of ways of expressing thoughts, feelings, and intentions, so brace yourself.

With businesses spanning the globe, working with people from a variety of cultures is the new norm. Unless you become culturally fluent and demonstrate respect for others – you're doomed.

Before diving into the detail of how to shake hands in the Middle East or whether you should bow to or kiss your colleagues, consider the following questions when thinking about culture.

Below are some reflections on body language that will keep you from making the dreaded faux pas when dealing with different cultures. Be advised that for reasons of space, this list is not exhaustive.

Facial Expressions

While facial expressions denoting happiness, sadness, anger, disgust, fear, and surprise are similar worldwide, the intensity of expression varies from culture to culture.

In **Asian** cultures, facial expressions are suppressed because animated expressions are viewed as lacking in control and too much smiling is seen as a sign of shallowness. In contrast, **Latin and Arabic** cultures exaggerate their grief and sadness, while most **American** men hide theirs.

Smiling

While Western thinking would have you believe that the one, sure-fire expression for winning hearts and wooing minds is a *genuine* smile, the act of smiling is culturally influenced and is not a simple indicator of goodwill and bonhomie. For example, in **Latin and most Western** cultures, smiling is expected behaviour and a mark of appreciation, acceptance, and respect. However, in countries that are less emotionally expressive – such as **Japan, China, Switzerland, and Russia** – smiling is only shared amongst people who know each other. In many **Asian** cultures, smiling for no specific reason is considered insincere and a sign of foolishness. The **Koreans** have a saying: "He who smiles a lot is not a real man." **Russians** complain that **Americans** smile "as if they were plugged into the wall", while living by their culture's proverb: "To smile or to laugh without reason is a sign of idiocy."

Russians consider a polite smile as "the servant's smile", denoting a person's insincerity and unwillingness to show true emotion. The **Germans** also believe that Americans smile too much, and save their own smiles for true happiness. America is not the only culture that values the smile as a means of conveying good will. People from **Thailand** consider the smile to be the most appropriate gesture a person can give, and are ranked the people who smile the most.

As all successful diplomats know, smiling can ease relationships and is therefore their expression of choice.

Warning: If you come from a culture of smilers, take heed. Like many people from the **Far East**, the Japanese view Westerners' smiles as unattractive, showing too many teeth and too much gum.

A final thought about smiling: To further confuse the issue of smiling, people from **Eastern** cultures tend to smile when they're angry, sad, or embarrassed as well as when they're happy, which can be really confusing. In those cases, look to their eyes.

Eye Contact

The eyes are the gateway to the soul. Look to them for honing in on someone's feelings, thoughts, and intentions. Because **Asian** cultures value humility and the suppression of emotions, they rely on the eyes for communicating messages rather than turning to the mouth.

In the **UK, USA, Australia, and Western Europe**, eye contact is expected as a sign of interest and engagement. In addition, strong eye contact projects an air of confidence. A lack of eye contact is considered aloof, unresponsive, or apathetic. *Beware of engaging with too much eye contact.* When you're speaking, focus on an individual's eyes no more than 65% of the time. When you're listening, you can look a little longer, not surpassing 85% of the time. Any more than either of those two percentages can make you appear threatening, if not just a bit odd.

In **Hispanic, Asian, Middle Eastern, and Native American** cultures, eye contact is thought to be disrespectful, discourteous, and just plain rude. These cultures tend to be authoritarian, and discourage anyone making steady eye contact with those who are considered to be their superiors. People from these cultures often look away from you when engaging in conversation. Women may especially avoid eye contact with men, because it can be taken as a sign of sexual interest. Long-held eye contact between two people of the same sex is a way of demonstrating honesty, sincerity, and seriousness.

Although **African and Latin American** cultures are different in many ways, they are both strong hierarchical societies. Intense eye contact is interpreted as antagonistic, hostile, and downright belligerent.

Physical Contact

As a general rule, cultures with high emotional restraint concepts, including the **English, Germans, Scandinavians, Chinese, and Japanese**, refrain from physical contact in public. People who encourage the expression of emotion, such as **Latinos, Middle-Easterners** and those of the **Jewish** faith, expect physical contact as part of normal conversation.

In most **Western** countries, physical contact means social dominance. Higher-status people tend to initiate physical contact, while people of lower rank are at the receiving end.

 LOOK, DON'T TOUCH

When I was a young woman working as a journalist, my older male boss would frequently come by my desk, place his hand on my shoulder, and lean over me to read what I had written. Every time he touched me I felt uncomfortable and wanted to slap his hand away. Had he been my peer, I would have. Because he was my boss, I had to tolerate his behaviour. A big cheer now that kind of behaviour can get a person thrown in jail.

Hugs, hand-holding, and cheek-kissing are normal forms of greeting the same gender in the **Middle East, Latin America, and southern Europe**, and other casual forms of physical contact during the course of conversation are to be expected. On the contrary, woe betide the person who accidently brushes up against a **northern European or Scandinavian**. Like the **Japanese** and **Chinese**, people from these cultures do not appreciate touching or being touched, although they don't take the extreme action of bowing in greeting and departure as their Asian cousins do.

While cheek-kissing is seen as a normal form of greeting in some cultures, other cultures do not appreciate touching or being touched.

Muslims have strict cultural rules about physical contact. Men and women are forbidden to do this, even casually, in public and it is rare to see couples, including those who are married, holding hands when other people are around.

When doing business in the **Middle East**, handshakes are customary and can last a long time. Wait until the other person has withdrawn their hand before withdrawing yours. If you are a man being introduced to a woman, wait until she offers her hand in greeting. If she doesn't, you don't either. Initiating physical contact with a woman and making prolonged eye contact is frowned upon.

In **Asia**, never touch a person on their head. Not even a child. The head is considered to be sacred territory, housing the soul. To touch a person on their head puts their soul in jeopardy. In addition, should you find yourself in **Vietnam** in the presence of a beautiful baby, remain silent. Although your instinct is to admire the child, refrain. The Vietnamese believe that commenting on a baby's cuteness will be overheard by evil spirits who will see that harm comes to the child.

People from **India, Africa, and the Middle East** always use their right hand for greeting, touching, and eating. They consider the left hand to be unclean as it is reserved for personal hygiene and using it in public is a social insult. When eating in **India**, break your bread with your right hand only.

Gestures

Crossing your legs in the **Middle East, Asia and South Africa** in such a way as to show the sole of your foot is considered rude and offensive, as the gesture is a sign of ill will or a bad omen. In Japan, never cross your legs in the presence of someone older or more respected than you.

In **Western** cultures the "thumbs up" gesture is a sign of satisfaction, whereas in **Middle Eastern** countries the gesture is highly offensive.

A "thumbs up" may be a positive sign in some countries, whereas it is considered highly offensive in others.

When it comes to shaking hands, in **North America** a handshake demonstrates that the deal is sealed and negotiations are complete. In the **Middle East** a handshake is a sign that you've been accepted and that serious negotiations are about to begin.

In most cultures pointing is impolite, so don't do it. If you must gesture towards someone or something, gesture with an open palm.

Gesture with an open palm, rather than pointing.

Vocal Patterns

Laughing, crying, yelling, and belching send different messages in different cultures. In the Far East, including **Japan and South Korea**, giggling indicates embarrassment while in **India**, belching signals satisfaction. A loud voice in **Arab** cultures indicates strength, while a soft voice is a sign of weakness. **Germans** perceive a loud voice as a sign of confidence and authority, while the **Thais** consider it to be impolite and the **Japanese** perceive it as a loss of control. No wonder there's so much confusion in the world!

Space

Personal space is the distance you maintain between yourself and another person, and protocols vary widely across cultures. In the **UK, USA, and most of Europe**, people are most comfortable keeping one to two metres' space between family and friends and up to three metres between strangers and business associates. Throughout the **Middle East, China, and Asia**, people are comfortable getting up close and personal as they are used to having less personal space than Westerners.

> "Culture is the widening of the mind and of the spirit."
> –Jawaharlal Nehru

The world is a big place, with many different forms of acceptable behaviour. When engaging with people from cultures different from yours, take a considered approach. If you're unsure how to behave and haven't had time to research it, observe the locals. Follow their lead. Go slowly, tread lightly, and treat cultural conventions with respect.

EXERCISE

To broaden your empathy, imaginative sympathy, and cultural outlook, learn about a culture different from yours. Perhaps one that you're doing business with. Ask yourself the following questions:

- What values does this culture embrace? How is it similar to/different from yours?
- How do people conduct relationships and display emotion?
- What are the social rules and boundaries with regard to gender?
- How does this culture relate to and display authority?
- How do people in this culture communicate? How direct/indirect are they in expressing their thoughts and emotions?

Before doing business in cultures different from yours, I highly recommend visiting www.argonautonline.com. I also encourage you to read the work of Fons Trompenaars, Charles Hampden-Turner, Edward T. Hall, Richard D. Lewis, and Geert Hofstede for furthering your cultural awareness. In addition, my book *Communication Skills For Dummies* has an excellent chapter on how to communicate across cultures with elegance, effectiveness, and ease.

A QUICK GUIDE TO FINDING OUT ABOUT SOMEONE WITHOUT ASKING

"Life isn't about finding yourself. Life is about creating yourself."

George Bernard Shaw

Pay attention to the way people behave if you want to find out about them. By observing

- facial expressions
- gestures
- vocal patterns
- posture

you discover the person within.

Throughout this book we have been looking at the non-verbal behaviours that reveal a person's thoughts, moods, and intentions. Here's a handy list to help you interpret what you see and hear. Before making an assessment, always consider the context and look for clusters of gestures.

Facial Expressions

Negative	Positive
FOREHEAD	
• Tight and wrinkled • Muscles pulled down and towards centre • Lowered eyebrows	• Relaxed and smooth • Muscles released out and upwards • Raised eyebrows
EYES	
• Contracted pupils • Scowling • Squinting • Staring • Glaring • Avoiding eye contact	• Enlarged pupils • Muscles lifted around eyes • Open eyes • Soft gaze • Warm expression • Seeking eye contact
MOUTH	
• Muscles pulled down • Pursed lips • Frowning • Chewing or sucking on lips	• Muscles lifted • Relaxed lips • Smiling • Lips calm

Negative	Positive
SKIN TONE	
• Heated • Perspiring • Flushed	• Cool • Dry • Steady colour

Gestures

Negative	Positive
HEAD	
• Chin thrusts upwards • Chin hangs downwards • Forward tilt to show disapproval • Shaking from side to side in displeasure and censure • Turning away from	• Chin slightly raised • Chin rests horizontally • Side tilt to show interest • Nodding in agreement, encouragement, approval • Turning towards
HANDS	
• Clenched fist • Fingers pressed tightly together • Pointing, jabbing with finger • Finger drumming • Wringing hands • Hands gesturing above shoulder height • Fist slamming	• Open hand • Fingers relaxed • Whole hand indicates • Still fingers • Forward and upward-facing palms • Hands gesturing between mid-chest and waist height • Fingers in steeple position
ARMS	
• Crossed • Held close to body • Hanging limply by sides	• Uncrossed • Held slightly away from body • Bent elbows at waist level, fingertips touching in front of body
FEET	
• Shuffling • Jiggling • Tapping toes • Pointed away from speaker	• Firmly placed beneath body • Still • Pointed towards speaker

(Continued)

(Continued)

Negative	Positive
MOVEMENTS	
• Short • Sharp • Jerky • Tentative	• Even • Smooth • Fluid • Assured
SPATIAL AWARENESS	
• Too close/far away	• Appropriate distance

Vocal Patterns

Negative	Positive
• Dull • Flat • Monotonous • Grating • Harsh • Too loud • Overly soft • Snarling • Whining • Quivering • Mumbling • Short, shallow breaths • Derogatory language • Long, rambling sentences • Fast paced • Slow and laborious • Timid or bombastic	• Bright • Vibrant • Varied • Smooth • Rich • Appropriate volume • Easy to hear • Warm tones • Resonant • Solid • Clear articulation • Long, deep breaths • Complimentary language • Clear and concise • Measured • Quick and easy • Confident and compelling

Breathing Patterns

Negative	Positive
• Short • Shallow	• Deep • Calm

Posture

Negative	Positive
• Slumped • Shoulders hunch forward • Chest caves in • Chest thrust forward, back sways • Pulling away from • Unbalanced	• Upright • Shoulders relax back and down • Chest expands • Chest is open, back is vertical • Leaning in towards • Balanced

Appearance

Negative	Positive
• Badly fitting clothes • Poor sense of style • Dirty hair • Bad haircut • Poor dental habits • Bitten fingernails • Over/underweight • Poor fitness	• Properly fitting clothes • Dresses appropriately • Clean hair • Suitable haircut • Goes to the dentist regularly • Manicured nails • Appropriate weight for age and body type • Exercises often

"The human body is the best picture of the human soul."

–Ludwig Wittgenstein

ABOUT THE AUTHOR

 Elizabeth Lindsay Kuhnke is an Executive Coach, specializing in impact and influence. An acknowledged expert and best-selling author on the subject of communication and non-verbal behaviours, Elizabeth works with senior leaders and rising stars in global organizations, helping them present themselves at their authentic best with clarity, confidence, and commitment.

A former actor, Elizabeth holds advanced degrees in speech, communications, and theatre arts. She is frequently quoted in the international press and appears on television and radio addressing the subjects of confidence and non-verbal behaviours. A popular and highly entertaining conference presenter, Elizabeth regularly participates in continuous professional development and holds several coaching qualifications. She espouses treating people with respect and developing rapport in order to produce outstanding results.

Elizabeth is married, has two grown-up children and a black miniature poodle named Humphrey. Clients and colleagues have compared her with: a pit bull terrier, because she stands her ground; a radiator, because she generates warmth; and an Olympic athlete, because she never gives up. Elizabeth was recently presented with the Sue Ryder Women of Achievement Award for her work in the charity sector.

ACKNOWLEDGEMENTS

When Capstone invited me to write this book I jumped with joy. Literally. Big grin on my face. Even fist-pumped. Since early childhood, non-verbal behaviour has fascinated me and has continued to do so throughout my life.

I would like to thank the following individuals for their contributions to this book. Without them, you wouldn't be reading this:

1. The talented, dedicated, and patient team of editors and support staff with whom I've had the privilege of working on this project.
2. Clients and colleagues, who unfailingly provide content and continuously inspire me.
3. My father and late mother for serving as great role models.
4. Friends and relatives for challenging and encouraging me.
5. You, the reader. For showing an interest and wanting to communicate at your very best.
6. Hellmuth, Kristina, Max, and Humphrey for hanging in there. Even when my body language indicates that I'm in a mood, their open facial expressions and welcoming gestures reassure me that everything's going to be all right.

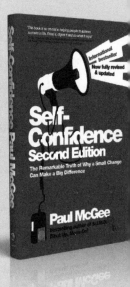